T0339910

.

Taiwan and the Changing Dynamics of Sino–US Relations

Wang discusses the dynamics of Sino–US relations since 2008 and the implications for relations between Taiwan and both the United States and the People's Republic of China.

Ever since China surpassed Japan to become the world's second largest economy, it has appeared to shift its policy shift from "biding our time" and a self-described "peaceful rise" toward increased assertiveness in regional and international affairs. This has only become more pronounced since the 19th Party National Congress in October 2017, when Xi Jinping reiterated his agenda for "the Chinese Dream." In contrast, the US's "Pivot to Asia" strategy has been widely perceived as unsuccessful. In its precarious political position between China and the United States, Taiwan is especially exposed to the fluctuations in policy and diplomatic relations between the two powers. The three bilateral relationships are intertwined, with policy changes and actions in any one of them affecting the other two. Wang emphasizes the "small power" and "disputed nation-state" perspective of Taiwan, over the "great power politics" of the United States and China. In doing so, he presents an analysis of how the changing dynamics of Sino–US relations and the great power transition in Asia have an impact on smaller stakeholders in the region.

A valuable resource for scholars and policy-makers with a focus on Taiwan's position in Sino–US relations.

Hung-Jen Wang is Professor of Political Science at National Cheng Kung University, Taiwan. He is currently also the Secretary-General at the Taiwan Society of Japan Studies (TSJS).

Politics in Asia series

Decolonizing Central Asian International Relation
Beyond Empires
Timur Dadabaev

Russia in the Indo-Pacific
New Approaches to Russian Foreign Policy
Gaye Christoffersen

China and Human Rights in North Korea
Debating a "Developmental Approach" in Northeast Asia

The Volatility and Future of Democracies in Asia
Hsin-Huang Michael Hsiao and Alan Hao Yang

Chinese Election Interference in Taiwan
Edward Barss

Japanese Public Sentiment on South Korea
Popular Opinion and International Relations
Edited by Tetsuro Kobayashi and Atsushi Tago

Taiwan and the Changing Dynamics of Sino-US Relations
A Relational Approach
Hung-Jen Wang

Dictionary of the Modern Politics of Southeast Asia
Joseph Chinyong Liow

For more information about this series, please visit: *www.routledge.com/ Politics-in-Asia/book-series/PIA*

Taiwan and the Changing Dynamics of Sino-US Relations

A Relational Approach

Hung-Jen Wang

Routledge
Taylor & Francis Group

LONDON AND NEW YORK

First published 2022
by Routledge
4 Park Square, Milton Park, Abingdon, Oxon OX14 4RN

and by Routledge
605 Third Avenue, New York, NY 10158

Routledge is an imprint of the Taylor & Francis Group, an informa business

© 2022 Hung-Jen Wang

British Library Cataloguing-in-Publication Data
A catalogue record for this book is available from the British Library

Library of Congress Cataloging-in-Publication Data
A catalog record for this book has been requested

ISBN: 978-1-138-59813-3 (hbk)
ISBN: 978-1-032-22883-9 (pbk)
ISBN: 978-0-429-48661-6 (ebk)

DOI: 10.4324/9780429486616

Typeset in Times New Roman
by Apex CoVantage, LLC

Contents

Illustrations

Preface

In June 2017, I received an email from Simon Bates, who introduced himself as a Singapore-based Routledge editor for social sciences and history. He expressed his interest in a paper I had authored on China–US–Taiwan relations that was presented at an International Studies Association (ISA) conference in Hong Kong. Over the next few months, we had several discussions about the content of a possible book on the same topic. After signing the publishing agreement, I had a brief but strong feeling of panic: was I being foolhardy in accepting an assignment to write a book on relations among the three countries in the aftermath of Donald Trump's victory in the US presidential election? How was I to figure out the new foreign policy of an administration that had such little expertise in diplomatic relations?

While preparing the manuscript, I continued to feel frustration. I was faced with the task of understanding the new administration's strong anti-China position while at the same time considering the possibility that President Trump might use Taiwan as a bargaining chip to win concessions from the Chinese side. A small but significant number of policy-makers and researchers expressed fear that Taiwan might be "sold" to China by the United States, but it never happened. Since President Joseph Biden took office, the United States has taken tougher positions on issues involving China and has given evidence that it considers Taiwan's security as an important aspect of US interests in the Indo-Pacific region.

This book is one of many efforts to catch up with the dynamic, opaque, and uncertain details of relations among China, the United States, and Taiwan. This volume is different in that it uses the concept of relationality to understand the situation, and in this respect, I am indebted to Professor Chih-yu Shih of National Taiwan University. He taught me how to incorporate the concept of balanced relations into my approach to IR—an alternative way to understand the behaviors of state actors and to challenge conventional IR concepts such as power and self-interests. It is my hope that this book makes a worthwhile contribution to a new understanding of international politics, with relations occupying a central position.

I also wish to thank National Cheng Kung University, the Taiwan Ministry of Science and Technology, and the Taiwan Ministry of Foreign Affairs for their financial support as I conducted the research for this manuscript. Finally, I am grateful to my wife, Joan Yang, for her tolerance of my many long absences from home to conduct interviews and write in my campus office. Thanks also to my parents and the many friends who have given me support while asking for little in return.

Hung-jen Wang
September 20, 2021
Department of Political Science
National Cheng Kung University
Taiwan

1 Introduction

Goals

The primary goal for this book is to review and add detail to the changing dynamics of Sino–US relations since 2008, when the People's Republic of China hosted the Summer Olympic Games for the first time. This event was followed by a period of rising national confidence in the country's international status. It is considered a turning point in China's relations with its Asian neighbors (especially the Philippines and Japan) and Western countries (especially the United States). Those neighbors and countries rejected China's "harmonious world" propaganda efforts, preferring instead to adhere to an image of China as a long-term threat. Against this backdrop, I will consider different approaches to understanding dynamic relations between the two major powers, with Taiwan playing a secondary but pivotal role in both Chinese and US identity, as well as in building relations. I will consider implications for challenges to mainstream international relations (IRs) theory building in general and Taiwan's relations with both China (commonly referred to as cross-Strait relations) and the United States in particular. The literature contains many analyses of bilateral dealings involving these three countries, most of them addressing the impacts of Washington–Taipei or cross-Strait relations on Sino–US relations and vice versa. Clearly, any effort to explain one of the three bilateral relationships must also consider repercussions within this triangular framework.

In this investigation of bilateral relations in the Asia-Pacific region, a relational approach will be used to explain their effects on Taiwan's pursuit of its own interests, as well as the regional and international security contexts that sustain the country's domestic political and societal development. Thus, the guiding question for this book is "What are the implications of the current confrontational state of Sino–US relations for the future of Taiwan's strategic role in the Asia-Pacific region, on its engagement with China and

DOI: 10.4324/9780429486616-1

the United States, and on the maintenance of stability in East and Southeast Asian countries?"

We are just beginning to access an understanding of the power transition between China and the United States that has evolved over the past two decades. Since the mid-1990s, we have had a front-row seat for watching China's expansion to become the world's second largest economy, replacing Japan in 2010. At the same time, we have watched China shift from a self-proclaimed image as a peacefully rising power, to one of "biding its time," to one of asserting itself in regional and international political affairs. These transitions have been marked by events such as China's sovereignty claims on disputed islands in the South China Sea and increasingly sharp diplomatic criticism of the West (especially the United States) for what it claims are unfair and discriminatory practices—note especially China's reactions to criticisms and suspicions associated with the COVID-19 pandemic.

There is no shortage of ideas or scenarios to consider when identifying or debating factors that have contributed to the current tensions in international politics involving China—for example, the ways that strongman practices emerging under Xi Jinping resemble those of Mao Zedong during the Cold War era, with the new leadership pursuing a national agenda that emphasizes the so-called "Chinese Dream" while constantly reminding all citizens of their national history of being bullied and oppressed by Western imperialism and hegemonism. Chinese are regularly encouraged to view themselves in response to images and actions promulgated in the West. At the same time, we are witnessing a lack of consistency in America's Asian policy, beginning with an ambitious "Pivot to Asia" strategy during Barack Obama's first term, a weakening of that strategy during his second term, a return to an Indo-Pacific strategy emphasizing strong assertions of power during the Trump administration, and (at the time of this writing) a yet-to-be defined Biden administration strategy. Given the dramatic changes in domestic politics in both China and the United States over the past decade, with all movements and policy changes influencing regional as well as global security and stability, anyone addressing these issues must pay attention to constantly and rapidly changing trends before getting involved in the risky task of predicting problems that are likely to emerge.

Learning to interpret dynamic changes in relations and the ways that they are likely to shape our long-term understanding of and reactions to certain facts is required to understand a new IR rationality that does not necessarily adhere to the logic or rules that have long been taught by Western IR theorists. Thus, instead of accepting great-power politics as its guiding principle (as is the case in many textbook descriptions of IR and security issues), this volume will look at evolving regional security issues from a relational perspective, one that emphasizes the constitutive role of Taiwan's "small power" or its "disputed nation-state" status in reference to China and the United States. In its dealings with two major powers, Taiwan regularly addresses regional and international issues under the gaze of a Chinese government that is steadily projecting a less-friendly image. Domestically, while the cross-Strait policy of former Taiwanese President Ma Ying-jeou appeared to be successful in establishing a harmonious and peaceful political atmosphere between the two sides during his first term, growing anti-China voices, especially among younger Taiwanese citizens, interfered with his intentions to promote certain trade agreements and to expand the two countries' general economic framework. The same anti-China voices became a base of support for current President Tsai Ing-wen's "maintain the status quo" approach, which views closer relations with or reliance on China as having great potential for hurting Taiwan's future national security interests. Both regionally and internationally, Taiwan is becoming increasingly marginalized due to Beijing's use of its economic power to persuade or threaten other countries to prevent Taipei from greater participation in global relations.

Taiwan's marginalized role is one result of a mix of external and internal factors. Externally, its disputed status as a sovereign state prevents it from participating in formal international organizations, especially the United Nations. According to Beijing's "one China" principle, Taiwan should be treated by all countries as a Chinese province rather than a nation-state. If you want to do business with China, you must accept this principle and reject any attempt by Taiwan to join international organizations. Pressure on countries to adhere to this principle has increased under Xi Jinping, causing nations to look the other way when Taiwan promotes its success in creating a democratically elected government marked by peaceful transitions of presidential power. Internally, Taiwan's economic power is still strong but suffering from a visible decline, and over the past decade, it has lost considerable economic sway to Japan and South Korea in countries such as Indonesia. The desire to regain market success in south Asian countries was the motivating factor behind the "New Southbound Policy" that the Tsai Ing-wen administration enacted in 2017. Its lack of initial success has been attributed to poor policy design and execution, but there have been signs of success following a period of adjustment.

The Relationality Literature: A Key Factor in Understanding State Behavior

This is certainly not the first book to analyze Taiwan's role in regional or international security issues nor the first to use the Taiwan example to understand the intricacies of great power politics. However, it differs from previous efforts by taking a relational rather than power- or interest-driven approach. By assigning an autonomous rather than dependent role to Taiwan, I will propose a new way of identifying and understanding the dynamic changes that have occurred over the past decade, as well as a new way to theorize Taiwan's role and relations with China and the United States. Relationality will be discussed as a contentious idea requiring user- and context-specific definitions to understand Chinese and American actions and to measure the extent to which the concept makes a theoretical contribution to specific studies of world politics and IR analyses in general. In previous articles,[1] I have argued that relationality is a useful tool for explaining how a Chinese worldview affects that country's policy-making decisions, especially compared to the themes of power politics and national interests that are dominant in Western (especially American) IR theory. Approaching relationality as an idiosyncratic product of traditional Asian or Chinese culture means overlooking the importance of the concept in the West, although with important differences in terms of logic and motivation. It is not my intent to deny the importance of power or self-interests in state behaviors, but to argue that their prominence is best viewed in the short term. Further, emphasizing a relational perspective means dealing with both positive and negative aspects of building relations. The efforts of many countries to establish economic connections with China represent an initial positive relationality, but with the potential to develop into a negative one in terms of financial debts and diplomatic demands. Further, China's relationship with the United States (especially in terms of trade) reflects a relations-building potential that deemphasizes cooperation in favor of disruptions.

Several articles and books on the relational turn concept are found in the Western IR literature. While viewed by some in the discipline as a "fringe" idea, it has also received support as a valid challenge to widely accepted realist and liberalist premises. Arguments considered implicitly or explicitly linked to the relational turn are found in "The Spread of Security Communities: Communities of Practice, Self-Restraint, and NATO's post-Cold War Transformation" by Emanuel Adler;[2] "Institutions and the Great Power Bargain in East Asia: ASEAN's Limited Brokerage Role" by Evelyn Goh;[3] "International Relations: A Network Approach" by Zeev Maoz, Lesley Terris, Ranan Kuperman, and Ilan Talmud;[4] "What's at Stake in the American Empire Debate" by Daniel Nexon and Thomas Wright;[5] "Network Analysis for International Relations" by Emilie Hafner-Burton, Miles Kahler, and Alexander Montgomery;[6] "Networks of Intergovernmental Organizations and Convergence in Democratic Economic Policies" by Xun Cao;[7] and "Relations before States: Substance, Process and the Study of World Politics" by Patrick Thaddeus Jackson and Daniel Nexon's,[8] among others.

Amitav Acharya and Barry Buzan's efforts to establish a research agenda for "global international relations" are considered an important progressive position. They have extended invitations for non-Western IR scholars to participate in a theoretical debate with members of the Western IR community in an effort to challenge the long-term dominance of Western (especially American) IR theorists.[9] In a 2016 issue of *International Studies Review*, Acharya and IR scholars from North America and other world regions called for the establishment of a global IR community whose views emphasize gender, the global south, international history, the concept of hegemony, and relational theory.[10] This book is based on the premise that these efforts to democratize IR represent an essential opportunity for new concepts, assumptions, and theories to be openly debated within the IR discipline.

IR scholars in Mainland China are eager to establish a relational theory research agenda that matches those found in the West. One of China's top political science journals, *World Economics and Politics*, has published articles on relational theory as it pertains to international politics.[11] Qin Yaqing has proposed three IR assumptions—a world of relations, the unity of knowledge and practice, and *zhongyong* dialectics—in support of a relational theory of world politics. Extracting relevant ideas from Chinese culture and recent Chinese diplomatic activity, Su Changhe argues that the Chinese tradition of "comprehensive understanding" is indispensable to relational theory and that relational concepts are acceptable substitutes for rational concepts when analyzing international politics. Wei Ling has examined how relations and networks can play effective roles in East Asian institutionalization processes, and Chen Dingding has used a processual constructivism framework to explain the complexity of and changes in Sino–US relations, hoping to make a contribution to the establishment of a Chinese IR school.

Two groups of Taiwanese scholars are engaging with Western ideas and lessons from Chinese civilization. One consists of history and IR researchers who represent a range of generations and research institutions. Led by research fellow Wu Yu-shan from Academia Sinica and professor Chen Hsin-Chih from the National Cheng Kung University Department of Political Science, members of this group are examining various pre-Qing periods of Chinese history in order to determine the extent to which premodern "international" ideas and diplomatic relations with non-Chinese can be meaningfully applied to modern discourses involving China. The second group, led by Professor Shih Chih-yu of National Taiwan University, is conducting research from a practical rather than historical perspective. Shih has developed a "balance of relationship" theory that he and his co-authors describe in two books: *Harmonious Intervention: China's Quest for Relational Security* (2014)[12] and *China and International Theory: The Balance of Relationships* (2019).[13] Shih is also the author of three full-length articles aimed at developing the idea of relationality: "Relations and Balances: Self-restraint and Democratic Governability under Confucianism" (2014);[14] "China's Quest for a Grand Strategy: Power, National Interest, or Relational Security" (2015);[15] and "Affirmative Balance of the Singapore-Taiwan Relationship: A Bilateral Perspective on the Relational Turn in International Relations" (2016).[16] Admittedly, these articles are exceptions with the relationality concept still in an early stage of development among Taiwanese academics.

Theoretical Motivation, Purpose, and Significance

There are three theoretical motivations for this book. The first is to clarify differences between both Taiwan and China and Western countries in terms of state behaviors based on existing emphases on power and self-interests, with the goal of challenging the idea that most Western IR theorists are wrong in their assumptions about China's actions, and to reconfirm their links to specific historical experiences and cultural traditions. The second motivation is to revisit practical aspects of Taiwanese and Chinese IR performance—neither can be considered exceptional in their attachments to sovereignty and core interests, but it is important to note that familiar Western IR terms such as *nation-state, sovereignty, national interests,* and *balance of power* have only recently been added to their IR lexicons. From a practical perspective, understanding relationality can help explain shifting Taiwanese and Chinese ontological positions (one clearly relational), as well as incentives underlying their participation in or withdrawal from individual systems. A third motivation is to respond to recent relational turn IR scholarship on topics such as the political practices of multilateral institutions. Chinese IR scholars such as Qin Yaqing and Su Changhe are engaging with some of their Western counterparts to develop research agendas based on relational theory and global IRs. In later chapters, I will discuss the premise that Taiwanese scholars must engage in this debate in order to keep up with their international peers and to prevent Chinese IR studies from being monopolized by either Western or Mainland Chinese interpretations.

In brief, a central goal for this book is explaining why relationality may be more useful than other concepts for understanding the details of China's participation in international politics, especially in global governance issues. Unlike Mainland Chinese IR scholars, I am not interested in establishing an ideal based on traditional Chinese philosophical or cultural practices. Instead, I will address relationality from the same practical perspective that the Chinese government is pursuing—that is, ambitious infrastructure projects such as "One Belt One Road" rather than active participation in Western-dominated multilateral institutions. In an effort to bridge the gap between modern and relational systems based on different ontological premises, this book represents a starting point for determining the possibility of these systems coexisting in parallel, as a hybrid, or interactively; for examining how China shifts between systems and ontologies; and for understanding how decisions to act according to one system or another are made.

Last, I will consider conventional Western political science concepts such as power, sovereignty, inter/independence, nationalism, and democracy as starting points for investigating relationality in Chinese global governance practices. Space limitations preclude an exhaustive review of these concepts, but a selective review is required to address questions such as why China was willing to confront two great powers (the Soviet Union and the United States) during the Cold War, but is now describing itself as reluctant to use the power that it is currently building. This question does not deny the many instances of rhetorical pushback by the Chinese government to criticisms regarding human rights violations and disputed territories. I believe that a large part of the answer involves the effects of relationality on rationality: this idea can be applied to China–US–Taiwan relations, with state actors focusing more on bilateral relations than on factors such as power asymmetry. In Western IR theory, power and self-interests are defined according to an anarchic world view in which states must constantly monitor the actions of other states in order to survive. The idea of relationality is a reminder that states also pursue security in their relations with other states. In this book, I will give examples illustrating this idea in dynamically changing relations involving China, the United States, and Taiwan.

The timing is right for a book that contributes to our understanding of international politics in general and China studies in particular, while avoiding an emphasis on power or national interests in favor of relationality as an epistemological lens. The timing is especially right in light of the "One Belt, One Road" initiative (which China is using to establish bilateral relations with countries in Central and Southeast Asia and Europe), China's creation of an Asian Infrastructure Investment Bank, and China's relations with other countries (especially North American and European) about its role and responsibilities in the COVID-19 pandemic. These are three of many examples of China's decreasing reliance on existing Western multilateral institutions and intentions to create new rules for uni-bilateral and multi-bilateral relations.[17] Thus, this book can be viewed as part of the dialogue between Taiwanese and Western IR theorists regarding China studies, one reflecting the idea that theoretical processes associated with IR and China studies should not be monopolized by a single entity. I believe it is important to critically examine and, in some cases, contest the claims of some Mainland Chinese IR scholars that a relational theory of world politics based on traditional Chinese cultural values is required as an act of separation from established Western IR theories. Instead, I believe the IR community needs to encourage a processual relationality based on mutual interactions among actors at a practical level, as well as skepticism toward assumptions regarding relationality.

Summary

The dynamics of Sino–US relations have never been more unpredictable or erratic. We are witnessing a global power transition marked by leadership changes in both countries, and China is clearly concerned about "educating" new political leaders in the United States on the delicate issue of the one-China principle—note the diplomatically awkward way that Donald Trump handled a congratulatory phone call from Tsai Ing-wen upon taking office. The existing dynamics serve as motivation for writing a book about how Taiwan might regain a degree of global visibility depending on how the Biden administration handles its relations with Beijing. I will offer a detailed examination of China–US, US–Taiwan, and China–Taiwan relations over the past decade for purposes of evaluating the ways that Taiwan might adjust its strategic position and express its self-identity as a small country dependent on the agendas of two great powers.

The rest of this book is organized as follows. Chapter 2 examines the American electorate's current pessimism regarding China in general and Sino–US relations in particular, and the potential effects of that pessimism on the Biden administration's China policy in terms of relationality. The chapter will address factors such as the failed expectations of democratic reforms in China and China's increasingly assertive foreign policy actions in the Asia-Pacific region. Chapter 3 discusses the idea that the Trump administration's lack of assertiveness in 2017 triggered a period of reexamining US–Taiwan relations according to a three-tiered bilateral/trilateral/multilateral framework. Whereas the Trump administration's emphasis on "America-first" interests favored a bilateral framework, the effects of a relational approach were more likely to be found in bilateral and multilateral frameworks that included negative references to China. Chapter 3 will also describe how uncertainties in the Trump administration's Asia–China–Taiwan policy could be viewed as a window of opportunity for Taiwan to manage its relations with the United States to its advantage. Chapter 4 looks at China's support for and resistance to UN charter reforms since the end of the Cold War, and the relationality dilemma that has resulted. The dilemma is explained in terms of two international roles that China feels pressure to fulfill that require different forms of relationality. Accordingly, China is sometimes perceived as acting in contradictory ways in its interactions with different states and international organizations. Chapter 5 examines decisions made by Xi Jinping following the 19th National Congress of the Chinese Communist Party, decisions that have increasingly projected an authoritarian image of governance that stands in stark contrast to the democratic values found in Taiwanese electoral politics. This is arguably the most visible of multiple differences standing in the way of consensus building. Chapter 6 looks at images and labels assigned by two leading American news magazines to China, Taiwan, and the United States between 1990 and 2018, especially during two peak years of crisis in cross-Strait relations.

Notes

1 Hung-jen Wang, "China's Assertive Relational Strategies: Engagement, Boycotting, Reciprocation and Press," *Issues & Studies,* 54(3) (2018), pp. 1–26; Chih-yu Shih, Chiung-chiu Huang, Pichamon Yeophantong, Raoul Bunskoek, Josuke Ikeda, Yih-jye Jwang, Hung-jen Wang, Chih-yun Chang, and Ching-chang Chen, *China and International Theory: The Balance of Relationships* (London and New York: Routledge, 2019); Hung-jen Wang, "Chinese IR Scholarship as a Relational Epistemology in the Study of China's Rise," *The China Quarterly,* 245 (2021), pp. 262–275.
2 *European Journal of International Relations,* 14(2) (2008), pp. 195–230.
3 *International Relations of the Asia-Pacific,* 11(3) (2011), pp. 373–401.
4 In Alex Mintz and Bruce M Russett, eds., *New Directions for International Relations: Confronting the Method-of-Analysis Problem* (Lanham, MD: Lexington Books, 2006), pp. 35–64.
5 *American Political Science Review,* 101(2) (2007), pp. 253–271.
6 *International Organization,* 63(3) (2009), pp. 559–592.
7 *International Studies Quarterly,* 53(4) (2009), pp. 1095–1130.
8 *European Journal of International Relations,* 5(3) (1999), pp. 291–332.
9 Amitav Acharya and Barry Buzan, *Non-Western International Relations Theory: Perspectives on and beyond Asia* (London: Routledge, 2010).
10 See *International Studies Review,* 18(1) (March 2016).
11 See *World Economics and Politics,* 10 (2016).
12 Chiung-chiu Huang and Chih-yu Shih, *Harmonious Intervention: China's Quest for Relational Security* (Farnham, Surrey, England: Ashgate, 2014).
13 Shih et al. (2019).
14 Chih-yu Shih, "Relations and Balances: Self-restraint and Democratic Governability under Confucianism," *Pacific Focus,* 29(3) (2014), pp. 351–373.

15 Chih-yu Shih and Chiung-chiu Huang, "China's Quest for a Grand Strategy: Power, National Interest, or Relational Security," *The Chinese Journal of International Politics,* 8(1) (2015), pp. 1–26.
16 Chih-yu Shih, "Affirmative Balance of the Singapore-Taiwan Relationship: A Bilateral Perspective on the Relational Turn in International Relations," *International Studies Review* (2016), pp. 1–21.
17 Chih-yu Shih and Hung-jen Wang, "Thinking Bilaterally, Acting Unilaterally: Placing China's Institutional Style in Relational IR," *China: An International Journal,* 17(1) (2019), pp. 151–172.

2 China–US Relations Pessimism in Light of Power-Detached Relationality

Introduction

This chapter addresses the impacts of increasing pessimism on Sino–US relations, especially in light of the summer 2016 ruling by an international tribunal regarding disputed territory in the South China Sea. I believe that deteriorating relations should not be viewed only as the result of a power transition between the United States and China but also a result of declining American patience about actively maintaining bilateral relations with China. Projecting a sense of impatience and taking a harsher approach in the name of protecting American interests were accepted and promoted by politicians wanting to be associated with Donald Trump's "America First" approach, but we are also witnessing a growing number of policy analysts and American China experts calling for a tougher approach in response to China's assertive behaviors and perceived intentions.

Another possible explanation for the loss of patience among American experts and policy-makers entails their disappointment over Chinese violations of the written and unwritten rules and practices of international organizations, which are considered fundamental for accepting China into international society and for successful multilateral relations with all Western countries, not just the United States. We are witnessing much less support for bilateral relationality between the two powers as China increasingly pursues a world view with Chinese characteristics. A strong example is Beijing's rejection of a ruling by an international tribunal in The Hague regarding China's claims to territorial and marine rights in the South China Sea—a ruling that challenges China's preferred approach to defining and controlling relations with other states. Another prime example is the expectation for all foreign governments to abide by the "one China principle"—a bilateral relationality that is being unilaterally imposed by China. According to this principle, Taiwan's ongoing efforts to establish a stronger partnership with Washington is a major factor in deteriorating China–US interactions.

DOI: 10.4324/9780429486616-2

It is generally acknowledged that Sino–US relations are not just about two states defending their respective national interests, nor are they constrained by a sense of unavoidable war as a rising power threatens to displace a dominant one. Instead, the relationship has broad implications for stability and the security interests of other state actors, especially in the Indo-Pacific region. Taiwan is only one of several nations concerned about Sino–US relations, the finer details of the South China Sea ruling, China's reaction to the election of a Democratic Progressive Party presidential candidate in Taiwan, and American politics. Against this background, this chapter will add one more aspect—relationality—to clarify the aforementioned concerns and explain how they drive the pursuit of security.

To understand how Taiwan might take advantage of deteriorating relations between China and the United States to advance its relational concerns, it is important to consider unconfirmed reports of Taiwan President Tsai Ing-wen seeking political support from Washington and Tokyo for purposes of gaining leverage in cross-Strait relations, which have undergone significant changes since Tsai replaced her Kuomingtang (KMT) Party predecessor, Ma Ying-jeou. Some Taiwanese analysts view deteriorating Sino–US relations as an exceptional opportunity for Taipei to enhance its diplomatic and strategic roles in the region, and supporters of Taiwan independence are excited about what they view as an opening for promoting Taiwan's international status.[1] This may appear to be a rational response for anyone who accepts the balance-of-power argument that small countries such as Taiwan have no choice but to align themselves with major powers. However, there is another way to view the situation: Taiwan is trying to recover the status and sense of autonomy from China that it has lost over the past two decades. According to a relational perspective, it is better for Taiwan to pull away from a worsening relationship with China instead of attempting to fix it. The United States is facing a similar decision in light of the failure of China to fulfill the fantasies of American political elites about Chinese democratic reforms. Should decision-makers in Taipei and Washington decide that their separate bilateral relationships with China are beyond repair and therefore require starting anew, their shared motivation would be based less on the perception of a power transition or loss and more on declining trust in China to keep its promises.

Concerns Associated with Incongruent Relationality Views

While being careful when using terms such as "pessimistic," "deteriorating," and "problematic," I must acknowledge that most of the foreign policy analysts I interviewed in the Washington, DC area during the summer of 2016 expressed strong concerns—in many cases, "worries" or "fears" would be more accurate—about future Sino–US relations, especially following China's emphatic rejection of the South China Sea ruling.[2] The views of some were in agreement with Harry Harding's analysis of American disappointment with China and his proposals for American policy revisions.[3] Similarly, David Shambaugh has commented on the pessimism toward and disillusion with China currently found in Washington think tanks—for example,

> the discourse in the American policy community underwent a notable shift in 2015. An unprecedented outpouring of commentary and reports spewed out of Washington think tanks that year and they were almost all negative in the way they portrayed China and U.S. policy towards China—all calling for a reevaluation of American policy, and most seeking a tougher policy across the board. . . . While China does its part to contribute to the fraying of ties, it must be said that there are some uniquely American sources of this deterioration. The disillusion with China America probably says much more about the United States than it does about China.[4]

These and similar comments from foreign policy experts and China watchers have received widespread attention and therefore will not be repeated in detail here. However, during my interviews, I heard several descriptions of how relationality and trust are affecting patience in American thinking toward China in terms of perceptions of improvement in bilateral relations and consequent policy revisions.

When looking at American and overall Western views on relationality, a growing number of English-language IR scholars are expressing concern over the ways that national actors are citing specific standards and preferences in the interest of self-restraint.[5] According to their observations, relationality entails a process in which individual states practice certain values, norms, and rules, which in turn strengthens the degree of relationality connecting specific groups of states while setting the stage for a long-term shared identity. Multilateral in nature, this type of relationality is established via processes involving self-practice, adherence to rules, and group socializing among nation-states.[6] The resulting obligations and community practices affect the ways that newcomers such as China interact with established communities, their institutions, and their rules. In theory, these institutions, rules, and practices are considered sufficiently strong to survive newcomer acceptance or rejection. As Harding notes, between Richard Nixon's 1972 visit to China and normalization of relations in 1978, the United States changed its long-standing policy of isolating China to one of engagement, integration, and assistance.[7] I interpret this change as an effort on the part of the United States to bring China into an existing practice community, with the expectation that according to the principle of relationality, China would accept those practices and act accordingly in order to establish and expand relations with the entire community.[8] As one of my interviewees explained, the United States established diplomatic relations with the People's Republic of China in hope of bringing it into the established Western order, but he also observed that if China had selectively chosen which practices to follow and which to ignore, or tried to alter the status quo or regional order, the United States would not have tolerated the situation for very long.[9]

Reviewing Sino–US diplomatic relations since Nixon's first visit, one finds multiple US efforts to understand and confirm China's true intentions regarding universally acknowledged rules governing multilateral relationality. But one also sees that Washington has repeatedly acted according to its own interpretation of relationality based on the aforementioned practice community, with ongoing expectations that China would understand and abide by those universally acknowledged rules. The United States may have viewed certain actions and events as implying China's willingness to do so: Deng Xiaoping's push for an open-door policy, rising domestic calls for *jiegui* ("to integrate," describing the effort to connect China's domestic market with Western/international markets) following the Tiananmen Square massacre, China's participation in international organizations in the 1990s, its World Trade Organization membership, and the 2008 Olympic Games held in Beijing. However, since 2010, there have been increasing complaints from Asian states regarding China's assertiveness in the region and requests for the United States to push back, thus putting its complex relationship with China to the test. From a relationality perspective, the American approach to dealing with China must be multilateral and therefore can only be considered valid when a set of community practices is maintained. The United States and other Western countries express anxiety whenever China violates international community norms or rules. Thus, the American approach to relationality is essentially epistemological in terms of the extent to which it uses international community norms or rules to understand and respond to China's foreign policy practices.

Most interviewees agreed with my suggestion that problems in Sino–US relations are not simply due to a power struggle between them but also due to their different views on rationality,[10] negotiation style,[11] historiography,[12] culture,[13] sensitivity,[14] regime type,[15] and the degree of openness in policy-making.[16] Recent domestic calls for injecting Chinese cultural practices into international politics reflect this list of concerns.[17] According to traditional Chinese thinking, all nations and nonnational actors are born to be related to one another, making it unnecessary for them to be related through practices.

According to this idea, China and the United States are destined to be related regardless of their different political systems, with expectations for mutual respect for each other's existence regardless of the ideological chasm that separates them. This perspective has deep cultural roots, beginning with the ancient tributary system that served as the basis for all relations between China and non-Chinese actors.[18] Today, its relations with others are based on a sovereignty system in which China and the United States are viewed as two parts of a larger self within which both hold equal power. Thus, if the United States interferes with Chinese sovereignty, it is considered an attempt to destroy the larger self, which naturally would strongly affect the United States at the same time.

Losing a balanced relationship would require China to focus on blocking further US intervention, including finding ways (possibly involving military action) to force the United States to the negotiating table. This explains, at least in part, Xi Jinping's call for a "new type of major power relations" during the Obama administration—that is, an attempt to establish a new and positive bilateral relationship based on mutual cooperation and respect. Due to strong concerns expressed by Japan, South Korea, and other allies and because Washington viewed Xi's proposal and related definitions as too ambiguous, it was rejected.[19] Xi's call may also be interpreted as China's way of reminding the United States of the details of their bilateral-and-reciprocal type of relationality, which is determined by their coexistence within the modern nation-state system. The Chinese perspective on relationality requires its counterparts to accept the existence of a larger consensus or identity and to acknowledge that all efforts to maintain mutual relationality should contribute to the formation of a larger collective identity—described as *daiwo* in Chinese, generally translated as "greater-self." However, it is important to remember that if the United States rejects Beijing's attempts to manage their bilateral relations in a "special" manner, then those relations can never be based on a specific form of Chinese relationality.

I believe that both forms of relationality—American epistemological and Chinese ontological—are responsible for creating an ambiguous and/or incongruent situation that prevents both from expressing patience, thereby encouraging short-term actions and responses.[20] According to an epistemological form of relationality, when international rules or values become internalized (resulting in an emphasis on concepts such as national interests), individual parties or communities may perceive a need to enforce international rules or values, even with nations that have no histories of them or inclinations to start practicing them. In such scenarios, a superpower or international community that feels most comfortable acting in accordance with rules created by established institutions must be willing to defend them to protect or preserve their identities—a poor framework for practicing patience. According to an ontological form of relationality, all nations are perceived as interrelated and therefore must accept responsibility for maintaining and defending a collective identity within a system that emphasizes stability. Thus, nation-states with very different political systems, cultural values, and historical experiences can still perceive themselves as related, with equal sovereign statuses and with respect for differences. In such contexts, any involvement in the domestic affairs of other countries represents a denial of their survival rights, thus damaging the entire system. According to a Chinese perspective, intervening in the domestic affairs of other countries simply cannot be tolerated.

Trust in Fulfillment and the Ability to Cause Harm

Several of my interviewees mentioned Thucydides's Trap—Graham Allison's description of a tendency toward war when an emerging power threatens to displace an existing great power as an international hegemon.[21] However, while most discussed power as an important consideration in deteriorating Sino–US relations, they refrained from going into detail about how power issues are contributing to that deterioration. Instead, when asked to comment on specific scenarios such as the South China Sea case, most gave nonpower reasons to explain why the American people, including researchers and analysts, are concerned about Chinese assertiveness in Asia. The potential for trust is reduced when such assertiveness is interpreted as harming the sense of relationality expected from "responsible states"—note the "responsible stakeholder" comment made in 2005 by then-Deputy Secretary of State Robert Zoellick regarding role expectations for China. According to this idea, the United States believes that China should acknowledge what kinds of decisions and actions must be taken in support of good relations. The idea also explains the discontent my interviewees expressed regarding the Chinese government's rejection of the South China Sea ruling from The Hague. Here are four excerpts from our conversations:

> While China has the [legal] right to claim sovereignty over those South China Sea reefs, China's claims have already violated internationally recognized values, and such behavior cannot be accepted by the United States.
>
> The reason why the United States is not happy about China's responses to the South China Sea ruling is because the Chinese government's behavior reflects an attitude of rejection and irreverence. Such an attitude makes Americans feel that China is still that undemocratic country that they've always had in mind.

What the United States and China's neighboring countries are disappointed about is not what China claims, since everyone is clear what it is, such as [an act in defense of] sovereignty, but how China has responded. . . . The Chinese attitude to reject the international ruling and what it did before the ruling have caused antagonistic feelings among others. . . . If the United States has any expectations of China, it is the hope that China can first establish its rule of law, and then democracy afterwards.

If China sees itself as a member of the international community, it should obey international rules as others do.

Another type of trust involves one party's belief that another has the capacity to hurt its interests, intentionally or not. Some interviewees commented on how the United States is treating China as a major threat in Asia, despite acknowledging that China may not have any intentions of replacing the United States in terms of its global roles. The following interview excerpts underscore the importance of "trust of capability" for China policy-makers:

In my view, the mistake in America's China policy is that the United States always thinks that China is continuing to expand its sea power, and the expansion is seen as threatening American security or interests. However, if we look at the reality, we know that China has no such capability or intention to expand its sea power to the Western Pacific island chains that the US is worried about.

Since 2012, I've found that China has shown many aggressive behaviors or actions that actually challenge America's national interests. According to the so-called American national interests, the US cannot tolerate a hostile power in Asia. Perhaps China is not reaching that level of hostility now, but no one knows if China will do so in the future.

According to my informants, the question of whether China has sufficient power to challenge the United States today is less important than its potential capacity. Unlike trust based on preassigned roles, there is a form of trust based on how one party objectively or subjectively perceives changes in another's material power. One interviewee insisted that Washington policy circles have always used the *idea* of China as a rising power as a reason to describe it as a threat. From a relationality perspective, if the United States continues to lose trust in China, it must consider radically altering the bilateral relationship—note the Trump administration's attempts to start a trade war and to create an anti-China alliance.

Can a Deteriorating Situation Encourage Greater Patience?

Patience is conditioned by one party's views regarding relationality and trust toward another.[22] After reviewing America's positions on relationality and trust, I believe that patience-motivated self-restraint or inaction on disputed issues is an option that should be considered as equally valid as the tough responses called for by a significant number of China experts in Washington. One reason is that perceptions of deterioration (either short or long term) are not based on structural factors normally viewed as constraining an actor's behavior, thereby encouraging—or at least not discouraging—unilateral policies of restraint based on the wishes of national leaders to maintain a minimal relationship with another state. Such policies would not eliminate the possibility of a harsher China approach based on balance-of-power motivations because self-constraint, no action, and a tougher approach all reflect different degrees of patience.

Table 2.1 shows how a mix of relationality and trust is influencing US patience toward China. As shown, incongruent views on relationality between the two states need to be readjusted in response to contrasting Western epistemological and Chinese ontological forms of relationality. Here, I will define adjusted relationality as a mutually accepted relationship that is continually adjusted or intervened by actors who are involved.[23] Unlike the Western form of relationality, the establishment of a mutually accepted relationship is not necessarily achieved via a practice community

Table 2.1 Patience in American policy toward China

Type of trust / Condition of relationality	Trust based on one party's judgment regarding the other's willingness to fulfill a predetermined international role	Mistrust based on one party's judgment of the ability of the other to cause harm to its interests
Incongruent views on relationality [lack of mutual relationality]	Integration [status quo: medium patience] Engagement [status quo: medium patience]	Balance of power [be tougher: low patience] Accommodation [strike a deal: low patience]
Adjusted views on relationality [progress toward mutual relationality]	No action on disputed issues [personalized relationship: high level of patience]	Self-restraint on disputed issues [personalized relationship: high level of patience]

because all actors are already considered connected—similar to a Chinese form of relationality involving a large collective identity or greater self. What differs (from the Chinese view) is that mutual relationality allows for a momentary degree of incongruity between actors that is open to modification as the decision-making processes of the two sides evolve. Since such incongruity might not be easily resolved or understood in the short term, a policy based on patience is required until better conditions emerge. This contrasts with China's calls for immediate responses to any and all interventions that it views as threatening to its sovereign status.

Trust is the most important aspect of a patience-based policy because it entails a tolerance of uncertainties that have the potential to affect a sense of mutual relationality. As mentioned earlier, American trust in China involves certain role expectations; therefore, expressions of trust can be misinterpreted as unilateral obligations that belie American-centric intrusions on Chinese sovereignty. The absence of high-level, easy-to-identify trust toward China carries the danger of being perceived as an effort to disrupt future power balances. I believe that trust in mutual relationality must be bidirectional, with both actors feeling obliged to exercise self-constraint on issues that seem unresolvable in the short term. Further, trust between any two nation-states is constructed on a foundation of personal relationships. One interviewee described the delicate tactics used during his time in the George W. Bush administration when establishing a strategic economic dialogue between China and the United States.[24] Similar high-level personal connections were rare during the Obama administration, which may have fed, at least in part, the current perception that Sino–US relations are worsening.

The Taiwan Question

In terms of power, Taiwan is often described as a small and weak state, but according to relational frameworks, it is considered an epistemological equal of the United States. Taiwan benefits from its willingness to practice democratic principles, free markets, and autonomy in civil society. It has built and maintained its relationality with the United States via ongoing democratization, reforms to its past authoritarian governance mechanisms, improved enforcement of intellectual property laws, transformation to a fairly unrestricted capitalist system, and peaceful power transitions between political parties, among other practices. It regularly receives commendations such as George W. Bush's description as "a beacon of democracy to Asia and the world."[25]

During an interview with an employee at the Taipei Economic and Cultural Representative Office (TECRO, which regularly sits in at high-level economic meetings with Japan, South Korea, and other Asian countries despite Taiwan's lack of sovereign rights), I heard an optimistic prediction that the country's relationships with the United States and others will receive fewer protests and interruptions by Mainland China over the long term. However, for the short term, Taiwan is unlikely to have anything more than a marginal voice in international relations; therefore, it will continue to serve as an example of how small-state diplomacy can still work when based on shared rules, norms, and values.

Still, the asymmetric power relationship that exists between the United States and Taiwan means that Washington will continue to exert considerable control over the country's general policies and to influence actual and planned actions on the part of the Taiwanese government. One of my interviewees described American appreciation for Tsai Ing-wen's promise to maintain the status quo in cross-Strait relations, but also emphasized the likelihood of Washington immediately asserting itself should she equate the status quo with Taiwan independence—a reality that confirms Taiwan's status as part of a grand American strategy rather than a sovereign equal. Clearly, Washington is not willing to stand idly by should Taiwan show signs of engaging in actions that might inflict significant damage on bilateral relations with Beijing.

In summary, Taiwan's expanding autonomy in deteriorating Sino–US relations should not automatically be interpreted as a result of closer ties with the United States or a product of cost calculations in American policy-making. A better analytical approach is to view Taiwan's rising status from a relational framework involving an epistemological connection with the United States. Increasing pessimism regarding America's China policy is best viewed as indicating a loss of patience with Chinese role expectations that are based, at least in part, on what the United States currently values and what Taiwan has already achieved in terms of democratic reforms. Thus, some of my interviewees see a future in which Taiwan will be able to take greater advantage of deteriorating Sino–US relations to pursue a *de jure* status as an independent entity,[26] since the underlying nature of Sino–US relations is not, as some theorists believe, a zero-sum power game.

Notes

1 Coen Blaauw, Executive Director of the Formosan Association for Public Affairs, interviewed on August 11, 2016.
2 Interviews were conducted with analysts, researchers, former diplomats, practitioners, and academic scholars during the summer of 2016. I wish to thank everyone who shared their insights on China–Taiwan–US relations. I also wish to thank Alan Romberg for his unselfish sharing of his personal network, Hana Rudolph for helping me with administrative tasks, and Antonio Liao for his

assistance during my time in the DC area. A list of interviewees and their affiliations can be found at the end of this book.

3 Harry Harding, "Has U.S. China Policy Failed?" *The Washington Quarterly* (Fall 2015), pp. 95–122.

4 David Shambaugh, *China's Future* (Malden, MA: Polity Press, 2016), p. 152.

5 Emanuel Adler, "The Spread of Security Communities: Communities of Practice, Self-Restraint, and NATO's Post-Cold War Transformation," *European Journal of International Relations,* 14(2) (2008), pp. 195–230.

6 Alastair I. Johnston, *Social States: China in International Institutions, 1980–2000* (Princeton, NJ: Princeton University Press, 2008).

7 Harding (Fall 2015), p. 101.

8 For example, a similar intention is found in Thomas J. Christensen's *Shaping the Choices of a Rising Power* (New York: W. W. Norton & Company, 2015).

9 Richard Bush, Nonresident Senior Fellow, Center for East Asia Policy Studies, the Brookings Institute, interviewed on July 20, 2016.

10 Stapleton Roy, Distinguished Fellow, Kissinger Institute on China and the United States, Wilson Center, interviewed on July 21, 2016.

11 Ling Chen, assistant professor of political economy, School of Advanced International Studies, Johns Hopkins University, interviewed on July 18, 2016; Michael J. Green, Senior Vice President for Asia and Japan Chair at the Center for Strategic and International Studies, interviewed on August 31, 2016.

12 Seth Cropsey, senior fellow & director, Center for American Seapower, Hudson Institute, interviewed on July 20, 2016.

13 Shihoko Goto, deputy director for geoeconomics and senior associate for Northeast Asia, Asia Program, Wilson Center, interviewed on July 14, 2016.

14 Douglas H. Paal, nonresident scholar, Asia Program, Carnegie Endowment for International Peace, interviewed on July 25, 2016.

15 Robert Sutter, Professor of practice of international affairs, the George Washington University, interviewed on July 26, 2016; Susan Lawrence, specialist in Asia affairs, Congress of Library, interviewed on August 25, 2016.

16 Jonathan D. Pollack, nonresident senior fellow, Center for East Asia Policy Studies, Brookings Institution, interviewed on July 5, 2016.

17 Yaqing Qin, "Relationality and Processual Construction: Bring Chinese Ideas into International Relations Theory," *Social Sciences in China,* 30(3) (2009), pp. 5–20.

18 Chih-yu Shih, Chiung-chiu Huang, Pichamon Yeophantong, Raoul Bunskoek, Josuke Ikeda, Yih-jye Jwang, Hung-jen Wang, Chih-yun Chang, and Chingchang Chen, *China and International Theory: The Balance of Relationships* (London and New York: Routledge, 2019).

19 Douglas H. Paal, nonresident scholar, Asia Program, Carnegie Endowment for International Peace, interviewed on July 25, 2016; Russell Hsiao, the executive director of Global Taiwan Institute, interviewed on July 27, 2016.

20 Patience is discussed in detail in a later section. In theory, when dealing with ambiguous situations the American electoral system encourages national leaders to have less patience in problem-solving compared to nonelected Chinese officials.

21 Graham Allison, *Destined for War: Can America and China Escape Thucydides's Trap?* (Boston: Houghton Mifflin, 2018).

22 See Chih-yu Shih and Hung-jen Wang, "Doing Without a Solution: Patience and Trust in Chinese International Relations," presented at the Fifth Global International Studies Conference, April 1–3, 2017, Taipei, Taiwan.

23 Ibid.

24 Dennis Wilder, managing director and senior fellow, initiative for US-China Dialogue on Global Issues at Georgetown University, interviewed on August 3, 2016.

25 Bonnie S. Glaser, "The Future of US-Taiwan Relations," Statement before the House Foreign Affairs Committee Subcommittee on Asia and the Pacific (February 11, 2016), available at http://docs.house.gov/meetings/FA/FA05/20160211/104457/HHRG-114-FA05-Wstate-GlaserB-20160211.pdf, accessed August 4, 2016.

26 This view is supported by at least two interviewees: Coen Blaauw and Michael Fonte, the latter director of the Democratic Progressive Party Mission in the United States, interviewed on August 15, 2016.

3 A Multilateral Framework for US–Taiwan Relations

An Interest-Detached Relationality

Introduction

Two electoral events affecting Taiwan–US relations took place in 2016: the Republic of China (Taiwan) elected Tsai Ing-wen, its first female president, and voters in Taiwan's most important international ally, the United States, put the unconventional politician Donald Trump in the White House. Afterward, the two countries went through a period of relationship redefinition and rebuilding according to the realities of an increasingly powerful People's Republic of China (China). Taiwanese international relations scholars are among many analysts using the US–China–Taiwan triad as an analytical framework for understanding bilateral US–Taiwan, US–China, and China–Taiwan relations.[1] A broad regional perspective is required when discussing topics such as America's general Asia policy, power politics, global competition involving China and the United States, Taiwan's position as a potential source of confrontation between Beijing and Washington, and the value of Taiwan in the eyes of American military strategists. Current US–Taiwan relations are evolving according to perceived and actual changes in both trilateral and asymmetrical bilateral relations involving the three countries.

In this chapter, I will discuss both the actual and lingering impacts of Trump administration actions and inaction on US–Taiwan relations. My views reflect information, ideas, opinions, and perspectives offered by research fellows associated with several think tanks located in the Washington, DC area, university professors, senior news reporters, staff members from both the PRC embassy and the Taipei Economic and Cultural Representative Office (TECRO), and congressional aides.[2] I will use this body of data to identify theoretical implications for Taiwan's future according to three levels of relations—US–Taiwan bilateral, US–China–Taiwan trilateral, and multilateral involving other members of the established global governance system. As part of this analysis (which was performed early in the Trump administration), I will show how the same observations help

DOI: 10.4324/9780429486616-3

to explain subsequent relationship development involving the three states. I believe it is incorrect to view that development according to converging or diverging national interests without also considering the assignment of specific actor roles or the function of trust.

China Policy versus Taiwan Policy

Understanding the impacts of Trump administration actions and inaction on US–Taiwan policy requires an understanding of how foreign policy was constructed on his watch—a challenging task due to the large number of unknown factors and lack of transparency throughout his term. Most of my interviewees wanted to give detailed answers to my questions but admitted that they really had no idea about what was going on inside the White House. Thus, a large part of my task as a researcher with a foreigner's perspective was figuring out Trump's leadership style, how and why various bureaucracies bent to his demands, and the content and tone of diplomatic communications originating from the Oval Office. Regarding the first question, I learned that President Trump was exceptionally sensitive to any attempt at controlling, monitoring, or managing his thoughts or actions. I was particularly struck by this September 2017 description of Chief of Staff John Kelly:

> While Mr. Kelly has quickly brought some order to a disorganized and demoralized staff, he is fully aware of the president's volcanic resentment about being managed, according to a dozen people close to Mr. Trump, and has treaded gingerly through the minefield of Mr. Trump's psyche. But the president has still bridled at what he perceives as being told what to do.[3]

A word that several of my interviewees used to describe President Trump's leadership style was "reckless"—a term synonymous with "rash," "hasty," and "unpredictable" and frequently used to describe Kim Jong-un, the North Korean leader. Trump's leadership style not only interfered with foreign policy stability and durability, but also increased the potential for the emergence of unexpected crises considered detrimental to the national interests of the United States as well as other countries. President Trump could tolerate such crises as long as they eventually produced new diplomatic relations he felt comfortable with. Certain foreign policy experts have emphasized the point that America's Asian allies dislike unpredictability and crave stability in US foreign policy, but they also acknowledge that Trump's unpredictability may have served as a deterrent against offensive actions taken by American rivals, especially Russia, North Korea, and

China. According to this view, relational stability is best applied to members of one's inner circle, whereas relational instability is a good strategy for pushing rivals toward preferred relational conditions.

As a researcher of American IR and political practices with a foreigner's perspective, I was surprised at President Trump's lack of self-restraint or willingness to compromise. My informants described him as consistently accepting "fixed ideas" and "wrong understandings" concerning major issues. Examples I heard included his suggestion to reconsider the one-China policy during his first month in office and the "bruising political style" with which he expressed his policy preferences.[4] When North Korea initiated aggressive acts involving long-range missiles and evidence of nuclear weapons development, analysts who viewed South Korea and China as potential sources of assistance dealing with Pyongyang were shocked when Mr. Trump went on the offensive and blamed both countries for failing to fulfill a poorly defined sense of duty. He also threatened to withdraw from the US–South Korea Free Trade Agreement and to order a probe of intellectual property infractions in China.

Another point made by many of my interviewees was the need to use bureaucratic clues when assessing Trump administration impacts on US foreign policy in general and US–Taiwan policy in particular. Several emphasized the point that almost 70% of top-level vacancies remained unfilled at the time of our interviews, including important positions in the State and Defense Departments considered relevant to Asian-Pacific affairs. Thus, Obama appointees serving as Acting Assistant Secretaries for the State Department's Bureau of East Asian and Pacific Affairs and Defense Department's Office of Asian and Pacific Security Affairs performed many of the duties of their former superiors with full awareness that they could be fired at any time for the simple transgression of being Obama leftovers. The experts I spoke with gave many other examples showing Mr. Trump's reliance on his inner circle while ignoring suggestions from qualified and skilled personnel. One argued,

> Whether US-Taiwan policy or US-China policy, it is supposed to involve many different bureaus or departments, and needs the deputy secretary level to integrate all different information or opinions into a core consensus or proposal, and then submit it to upper-level agencies to make policy suggestions for the President to consider. If the President makes some decisions regarded as improper by the bureaucrats, the latter are supposed to make objections. However, this is not how the Trump administration runs the government and makes its foreign policy.

Several analysts commented on President Trump's preference for bilateralism for rebuilding foreign relations, thereby overlooking the potential benefits of multilateral frameworks. Since the Trump administration never felt confined to a syncretized rationality signaling universal values or rules, it showed a strong tendency to consistently focus on individual bilateral issues. Depending on the observer's political preferences, that tendency could be interpreted as flexibility or inconsistency in foreign policy decisions. This underscores the presence of at least two types of relationality in international politics: bilateral and multilateral. As a rising power with specific cultural and historical concerns, China prefers bilateral relationality because it allows for greater control over individual others, regardless of inconsistencies across multiple bilateral relationships. In contrast, multilateral relationality, which has long been supported by Western countries such as the United States, fits with current global governance tendencies requiring the compliance of all participants with the rules and practices of regional and international organizations. The synchronized nature of multilateral relationality is viewed as beneficial for consistency in policy-making.

I was told by an interviewee that even though the Trump administration never consistently achieved a consensus on military and diplomatic strategies and policies, White House hawks clearly had strong influence in terms of economic policy. They were successful in convincing President Trump that it was in America's national interests to take hard-line approaches to both China and Taiwan on all economic issues, especially trade deficits—one expert emphasized the administration's definition of China as a "strategic competitor" rather than partner. While it is reasonable to interpret hawkish responses to China as driven by national interests, from a relational perspective the meaning of national interests is strongly dependent on whether China is perceived as a competitor or partner. I heard descriptions of President Trump as disliking China and Chinese on a personal level, which may have affected his views on national interests and questions such as the one-China policy—questions with significant potential for triggering conflict.

One of my interviewees suggested that President Trump had little, if any, understanding of issues involving Taiwan, which could explain why the country attracted little attention during his administration. However, this was an isolated opinion—other informants argued that the administration maintained an ongoing supportive position regarding Taipei. They noted that individuals such as Matthew Pottinger (a member of the White House National Security Council)[5] complained about prior bad experiences with China and were therefore supportive of Taiwan and its efforts to establish a democratic system of governance. I was also told by several interviewees that some people in the administration viewed Taiwan as crucial to

American interests in the Asia-Pacific region but primarily from a strategic-military perspective. One expert emphasized his perception of positive attitudes toward the new government in Taiwan as expressed by the State Department and the American Institute in Taiwan (the de facto American embassy), with expectations that such support would continue.[6] Further, almost all of my interviewees expressed a belief in strong bipartisan support for Taiwan in Congress, which had the potential to serve as a constraint against rash short-term policy decisions.

Bargaining Chips and Cross-Strait Relations

With so much stated and implied support from the US government and Congress, one might believe that Taiwanese should view themselves as beneficiaries of American protection. However, under Trump, that idea was open to challenge because the people in his inner circle never knew for certain what he was thinking at any moment. As President-elect, he willingly accepted a congratulatory phone call from Taiwan President Tsai in December 2016 but refused a second call after Chinese President Xi Jinping expressed strong displeasure over the first.[7] Another area of concern was the possibility of back channel communication between Beijing and President Trump's son-in-law, Jared Kushner—a very limited channel, but one that Taiwan apparently lacks. Experts familiar with the ways of Washington were clear about who they *should* talk to on issues involving Taiwan, but they were unsure about what to make of Jared Kushner. Several times I was told that a wait-and-see approach was demanded until some evidence of a comprehensive policy actually emerged. There is a much greater possibility of seeing such evidence during the Biden administration.

Another concern I heard is that the Taiwanese government's sense of reliance on the United States has become too strong. One informant reminded me, "Whether it is US China policy or US Taiwan policy, they're all based on America's own national interests, not on Taiwan's, China's, or others' interests." I believe that decision-makers in Taipei understand this and that in some areas, they perceive distinct differences between the two countries' national interests. However, I also believe that their actions and policy proposals will continue to be influenced by the optimistic belief that Taiwan's relational security is still strong and stable because the two countries share certain values that China rejects.

Taiwan's value as a potential bargaining chip is problematic on several levels. During the Trump administration, many Taiwanese contemplated a worst-case scenario in which Taiwan was abandoned in favor of an "America first"—motivated effort to build better relations with China. Most of my informants acknowledged the possibility of President Trump using Taiwan as part of a strategy to get China to exert greater influence over North Korea, despite considerable evidence showing that Beijing holds little sway over Pyongyang. There is a general agreement among analysts that following Tsai Ing-wen's congratulatory phone call, someone succeeded in explaining the importance of the one-China policy to President Trump. However, there is less certainty about whether his advisors were successful in persuading him to reject even the slightest inclination to use Taiwan as a bargaining chip. One expert told me that he never heard any reports of an American government official discussing the question of if or how Taiwan might be used to America's advantage in its relationship with China, an observation that can be interpreted in several ways. Whether true or not, there was a great concern in the diplomatic community during the Trump presidency that Taiwan might purposefully be used to support his self-perception as a talented dealmaker. However, any actions considered bad for Taiwan ran the risk of triggering such strong objections from Congress that Trump might have risked losing face—a scenario that he consistently avoided, although it depended in great part on which advisor had his ear at any moment.

To my knowledge, there was never a clear response from Trump or his inner circle on the question of what they thought about cross-Strait relations. My interviewees recommended that I read official remarks made by Secretary of Defense Jim Mattis and American Institute in Taiwan chairman James Moriarty. In a speech given at the Shangri-La Hotel in Singapore on June 3, Mattis mentioned three strategies that the Department of Defense was pursuing to achieve regional stability in East Asia. During his speech, Mattis said

> The Department of Defense remains steadfastly committed to working with Taiwan and with its democratic government to provide it the defense articles necessary, consistent with the obligations set out in the Taiwan Relations Act, because we stand for the peaceful resolution of any issues in a manner acceptable to the people on both sides of the Taiwan Strait.[8]

On July 13, AIT Chairman Moriarty made a clearer, if not stronger, statement in a talk given at the Center for Strategic and International Studies in Washington, DC. As part of that talk, he cited the text of the Taiwan Relations Act (TRA):

> It is the policy of the United States "to consider any effort to determine the future of Taiwan by other than peaceful means, including by boycotts or embargoes, a threat to the peace and security of the Western

Pacific area and of grave concern to the United States." It [the TRA] also asserts a US policy to "maintain the capacity of the United States to resist any resort to force or other forms of coercion that would jeopardize the security, or the social or economic system, of the people on Taiwan."[9]

Most of my informants expressed opinions regarding what they described as the "cold" relationship between Mainland China and Taiwan. They mentioned Tsai Ing-wen's efforts to show—with maximum good faith—how much influence she has over members of her own Democratic Progressive Party (DPP). As mentioned earlier in this chapter, President Tsai appears to be in favor in Washington based on her restraint and flexibility, leading some American analysts to describe China as unilaterally blocking substantial communication with Taipei and as putting excessive pressure on President Tsai to openly accept the one-China principle. I asked several interviewees about China's description of Tsai as upsetting the status quo by pursuing a "soft form" of Taiwan independence, and I was told that the US government saw little evidence in support of such accusations. Several emphasized their support for Tsai's right to govern her country as she sees fit, including the country's recent decision to separate the teaching of Taiwanese and Chinese history as different academic subjects—a practice viewed by China as evidence of "de-sinicization." One informant (who has a personal relationship with President Tsai) described her primary goals as improving the country's economy and preserving its international dignity; therefore, she avoids commenting on what she views as trivial matters such as the China/Taiwan history question. This same informant speculated that Beijing is too focused on the radical wing of the DPP and should instead recognize President Tsai's desire to satisfy the needs of a broad range of constituents. American analysts, including some of my interviewees, expressed skepticism about whether she actually needs to meet any expectations expressed by the Chinese government.

However, there is growing evidence that China has not only the intent but also the ability to pressure Taiwan to make changes in its favor, and some of my informants argued that Taiwan needs to improve its ability to push back against threats from the other side of the Strait. They note that the United States can continue to pursue the goals spelled out in the Taiwan Relations Act by selling arms to Taipei, but some are also expressing greater concern about Chinese President Xi Jinping's efforts to tighten his political, social, and economic control, to centralize his power, and to take a tougher stance on Taiwan. I heard concerns about his assumed desire to enhance his historical legacy by repatriating Taiwan.

Multilateral Relations and Asia-Pacific Policy

I also heard evidence indicating that Taiwan would receive more reliable support from the United States within a multilateral framework based on the Asia-Pacific regional order, which would allow the country to be treated as a strategic contributor to stability—an idea touching on the overlapping national interests of China and the United States. One informant argued that the United States was unlikely to use Taiwan as a bargaining chip because of its geostrategic location. According to this argument, there was little chance of the Trump administration giving China administrative control of Taiwan, and the Pentagon was unlikely to change its perception of Taiwan as part of its strategy to contain China as a potential military threat. I believe these suggestions, expressed in terms of national interest concerns, show that the basis for Taiwan's reliance on the United States is changing from material to relational concerns. It is worth taking a close look at the "port call" language added to the US National Defense Authorization Act for Fiscal Year 2018. The fine print seems to be more about how the United States can help Taiwan improve its defense capabilities than about simple port call procedures.[10] Some of my interviewees, including those who support a strong Taiwan–US partnership, viewed the port call idea as both reckless and risky for Taiwan, with few potential benefits for its defensive capabilities. While they openly supported the idea of the Trump administration helping Taiwan defend itself from possible attacks by China, they argued that the details needed to be expressed and executed properly, efficiently, and with minimum fanfare.

I heard two other reasons not related to national interests for closer Taiwan–US relations. The first is found in public statements concerning US commitments, not only to Taipei (in the form of the Taiwan Relations Act), but also to other Asian allies, especially Japan, South Korea, and Singapore. We are all aware of criticisms aimed at President Trump for being unrealistic in terms of asking Asian allies to accept greater responsibility for their own security. There were many media reports describing pressure on his administration to strengthen American cooperation with its Asian allies and to give assurances of enduring support for long-standing security agreements. Other experts emphasized the importance of Taiwan's liberal democracy. In the above-cited CSIS speech, AIT Chairman James Moriarty said, "Going beyond the Taiwan Relations Act, the mutual respect for democracy, human rights, and civil liberties also sustain the partnership between the United States and Taiwan."[11] In other words, there is agreement among many in Washington that it is in America's interests to support economic, military, and political success in Taiwan. American Asian experts who frequently travel to China and Taiwan often mention their affinity with the island country's political system and societal norms, which they emphasize over China's obvious economic advantages. Some interviewees commented on America's continuing expectations that one day China will enact democratic reforms, and the belief that Taiwan's democratic development during the past two decades proves that liberal democracy can coexist with Chinese cultural values—an assertion that Beijing rejects.[12] Some US experts are willing to openly express greater sympathy for Taiwan's *de facto* independence, which they believe has not received sufficient recognition from international society due to China's relentless pressure on other countries to support a "one China" policy.

Conclusion

Assessing the impacts of the Trump administration on US–Taiwan relations requires an examination of three relationship levels—bilateral, trilateral, and multilateral. Regarding its bilateral relationship with the United States, Taiwan occupied a special position because Donald Trump was exceptionally sensitive to domestic politics (e.g., negative attitudes toward China held by many of his supporters) when making foreign policy decisions. His tendency to personalize state relations diminished other factors such as abstract and imagined national interest concerns.

Although Taiwan has enjoyed strong bipartisan support in Congress over the past four decades, my informants complained about the lack of any clear access to Trump, the Oval Office, or high-level government officials for representatives from Taiwan to express their needs or concerns. Some experts I spoke with suggested that Taiwan should learn from Japan: despite the impossibility of a public visit to the United States by Taiwanese President Tsai, I heard suggestions for her to try using the media or business agents to communicate support for Trump's "America first" preferences in the same manner as former Japanese Prime Minister Shinzo Abe—that is, promote Taiwan as central to US national interests. Another suggestion I heard was for the Taiwanese government to do a better job promoting the country in the US media, since many US citizens—especially members of Trump's political base—do not understand why Taiwan is important to America's international strategy.

Compared to a bilateral context, Taiwan occupies a better relational position in a trilateral US–PRC–ROC context, with China's efforts to assert its power in the region seen as pushing the United States closer to Taiwan. Chinese President Xi made some efforts to establish a personal relationship with President Trump and pledged to work with the United States on certain narrowly defined issues, but with few lasting impressions or effects. China continues to do whatever it can to block the expansion of American influence in the Asia-Pacific region—note its attempts to assert complete control over navigation in the South China Sea and its loud protests against the establishment of a THAAD missile system in South Korea. China's apparent goal is to establish a "great power relationship" with the United States, a goal that does not require a trusting connection with Taiwan. President Xi continues to reject Taiwan's democratic practices—one of the most important factors determining American support. Sooner or later, Washington will have to find a balance between deteriorating China–Taiwan relations and its own strategic goals in the region. For this reason, a multilateral framework appears to be most advantageous for Taiwan.

Notes

1 This idea is tied to Lowell Dittmer's "strategic triangle theory" in "The Strategic Triangle: The Elementary Game-Theoretical Analysis," *World Politics*, 33(4) (January 1981), pp. 485–515. See also Wu Yu-shan, "Domestic Political Competition and Triangular Interaction Among Washington, Beijing, and Taipei: The US China Policy," *Issues & Studies*, 42(1) (March 2006), pp. 1–46.

2 Aides and assistants I spoke with included Collin Davenport, aide to Republican Congressman Jerry Connolly, interviewed on August 23, 2016; Guo-qing Zhen, secretary at the Taipei Economic and Cultural Representative Office, interviewed on July 21, 2016; Alan D. Romberg, distinguished fellow, Stimson Center, interviewed on August 10, 2016, and September 7, 2017; and Jim Heller, Director, Office of Japanese Affairs, US State Department, interviewed on July 31, 2019. A more detailed list of interviewees can be found in an appendix at the end of this book.

3 www.nytimes.com/2017/09/01/us/politics/john-kelly-trump.html?mcubz=0.

4 www.nytimes.com/2017/09/03/us/trump-north-south-korea-nuclear.html?action=click&contentCollection=Asia%20Pacific&module=RelatedCoverage&region=EndOfArticle&pgtype=article.

5 www.nytimes.com/2017/04/04/world/asia/matthew-pottinger-trump-china.html?mcubz=0.

6 Richard C. Bush, nonresident senior fellow at the Brookings Institute, interviewed on July 20, 2016.

7 www.reuters.com/article/us-usa-trump-taiwan-exclusive/exclusive-trump-spurns-taiwan-presidents-suggestion-of-another-phone-call-idUSKBN17U05I.

8 www.defense.gov/News/Transcripts/Transcript-View/Article/1201780/.

9 www.ait.org.tw/remarks-ait-chairman-james-moriarty-center-strategic-international-studies-csis/.

10 From the last paragraph of the Act: "Reestablishes regular ports of call by the U.S. Navy at Kaohsiung or any other suitable ports in Taiwan and permits U.S. Pacific Command to receive ports of call by Taiwan; directs the Department to implement a program of technical assistance to support Taiwanese efforts to develop indigenous undersea warfare capabilities, including vehicles and sea mines; and expresses the sense of Congress that the United States should strengthen and enhance its long-standing partnership and strategic cooperation with

Taiwan." See file:///C:/Users/hwang.STIMSON/Desktop/stimson/FY18%20ND AA%20summary2.pdf.

11 www.ait.org.tw/remarks-ait-chairman-james-moriarty-center-strategic-international-studies-csis/.

12 See L.H.M. Ling and Chih-yu Shih, "Confucianism with a Liberal Face: The Meaning of Democratic Politics in Postcolonial Taiwan," *The Review of Politics*, 60(1) (Winter 1998), pp. 55–82.

4 China's Position on UN Charter Reforms

A Relationality Dilemma

Introduction

This chapter examines China's evolving positions on United Nations Charter reforms since the Cold War era. It is important to look back at the Cold War to understand how China's responses to two great powers (the former Soviet Union and the United States) were driven by role considerations rather than asymmetric power differences—a situation that has some similarities with current China–Taiwan relations. In any present-day conversation regarding UN charter reform, China portrays itself as representing the interests of Third World nations and rejecting what it calls excessive interventions by the United States and other powers, even to the point of possibly damaging its established relations with those countries. However, when China sees advantages in defending the charter in its current form, it uses language expressing a desire to prevent the reemergence of Western imperialism. In sum, imagined acts of repression on the part of Western powers mixed with memories of imperialist aggression are influencing China to use negative relational processes tied to past acts of victimization and current fears of interference in internal affairs.

In the current IR literature, this is a generally overlooked aspect of the relationality-building process involving China and Taiwan. Since China's motivations and goals for supporting or resisting UN reforms are associated with its general role in international society and its specific standing in UN affairs, it is important to study negative relational processes as an important aspect of China's overall strategic policy. China has never held back from expressing its opinions on issues addressed by the United Nations, even before it became a member. Beijing has always criticized the United Nations as being monopolized by Western imperial powers and thus in need of reform, but it occasionally expresses support when calling for actions to strengthen the body's organizational functions. It all depends on China's strategic purposes.[1]

DOI: 10.4324/9780429486616-4

China's Political Concerns

The UN charter provides two paths for amendment: Article 108, which allows members to revise specific sections, and Article 109, which supports member efforts to review and change the charter in its entirety. Historically, China has frequently expressed its opinions on general UN principles, but in practical terms, it has tended to comment on specific charter sections rather than the entire document. An examination of its positions on UN reforms before and after its acceptance as a member state indicates regularly changing demands and goals. According to Chinese scholar Lei Zhao,[2] China's premembership (1949–71) focus was purely on political issues. This changed to economic issues during its early membership period (1972–89), and since 2005, it has emphasized a broad range of general issues such as peacekeeping actions, social development, and climate change. Chinese historian Dai-wei Zhu cites the first successful instance of amending the UN Constitution in 1963 (adding four nonpermanent member seats to the Security Council) when arguing that China played a positive role in influencing UN reforms and defending the legal rights of Third World nations even before it was accepted as a member.[3] Whether or not this argument is valid, it does illustrate China's long history of promoting and protecting its image on the global stage as a leader in the resistance against Western hegemonism and emphasis on power politics. Further evidence of this concern for defending Third World and developing countries is found in most public statements made before and after China's UN membership. According to this view, its relationships with Third World and developing countries and desire to prove its foreign policy legitimacy have served as guiding principles in all of its proclamations regarding the UN system in general and UN charter in particular.

There are many examples of China withholding support for UN actions, especially concerning issues that China perceives as politicized. In one example given by Suzanne Ogden, as early as 1955 "a leading Chinese Communist international legal expert, Ch'en T'i-ch'iang, even questioned the motives of the U.S. in proposing revision of the UN charter when it was 'beyond criticism.'"[4] Two other politicized premembership issues that invite closer inspection are Sino-Soviet Union relations and the legitimacy of the Republic of China (Taiwan) to hold the permanent "China seat" on the Security Council. In the early 1960s, UN members debated amendments to increase the number of nonpermanent Security Council members from 6 to 10 and total members from 11 to 15. The amendments were approved by the General Assembly on December 17, 1963, and went into effect on August 31, 1965. The then-Soviet Union rejected all ratification votes cast by the Nationalist China UN representative. According to Egon Schwelb, an attorney and ex-aide working in the UN Human Rights division and later a lecturer at Yale Law School:

> The Permanent Mission of the U.S.S.R. stated that the ratification 'by the Chiang Kai-shek clique . . . which represents no one and has no right to speak in the name of China' is illegal and contrary to the Charter of the United Nations (UN Doc. A/6031, Oct. 5, 1965). This was a continuation of the struggle the Soviet government had waged against the adoption of any Charter amendment in the absence of the Chinese mainland authorities through seven years from 1956 to 1963.[5]

An effort was made to amend Article 109 after the number of Security Council seats was increased.[6] The desire to make changes was based on perceived contradictory language between paragraphs 1 and 3:

> Paragraph 1: A General Conference of the Members of the United Nations for the purpose of reviewing the present Charter may be held at a date and place to be fixed by a two-thirds vote of the members of the General Assembly and by a vote of any seven members of the Security Council. Each Member of the United Nations shall have one vote in the conference.
>
> Paragraph 3: If such a conference has not been held before the tenth annual session of the General Assembly following the coming into force of the present Charter, the proposal to call such a conference shall be placed on the agenda of that session of the General Assembly, and the conference shall be held if so decided by a majority vote of the members of the General Assembly and by a vote of any seven members of the Security Council.

According to the position expressed by the General Assembly, both paragraphs state that "a vote of any seven members" in the expanded Security Council would be insufficient for establishing a UN charter review conference. Thus, the General Assembly wanted to change "seven" to "nine" and then submit the amendment for ratification by all UN members. The following is from the Assembly proposal, dated December 29, 1965:

> *Considering* that the Charter of the United Nations has been amended to provide that the membership of the Security Council, as provided in Article 23, should be increased from eleven to fifteen and that decisions of the Security Council should be taken, as provided in Article 27, by an affirmative vote of nine members instead of seven,

Considering that these amendments make it necessary to amend Article 109 of the Charter,

1. *Decides* to adopt, in accordance with Article 108 of the Charter of the United Nations, the following amendment to the Charter and to submit it for ratification by the States Members of the United Nations: In Article 109, paragraph 1, the word 'seven' in the first sentence shall be replaced by the word 'nine'.[7]

However, the Republic of China argued that Article 109, paragraph 3 should remain unchanged because measures that had been taken according to that paragraph were currently active; therefore, any deletion would cast doubt on its legal status.[8] Although the People's Republic of China obviously supported all objections raised by the Soviet Union to the legitimacy of the Republic of China to express any opinions on UN charter reforms, disputes between Beijing and Moscow during the 1960s blocked any expression of complete, unreserved support for Soviet plans or arguments made in a UN context.

Starting in the early 1960s, China expressed a perception of the Soviet Union and United States as acting in collusion to control the UN,[9] which resulted in its call for all UN member states to vote for a UN charter review, even though it had no legal standing. The effort failed[10] and tensions between China and the Soviet Union increased, even after China was admitted to the United Nation in 1971. The Soviet Union, France, the United Kingdom, and the United States all opposed a charter review for various reasons tied to their great power interests, leading Beijing to accuse Moscow as acting in accordance with the same "chauvinist-imperialist foundation" shared by other Western powers. The debate continued for four years. Tien Chin, the Chinese UN representative, made this comment at the 1,578th UN meeting held in 1975:

The majority of countries had advocated a review of the Charter. They had clearly pointed out that the purpose of reviewing and making necessary amendments to the Charter was to implement effectively the purposes and principles of the Charter, namely to ensure that the United Nations conformed to the tremendous changes which had occurred in the international situation and in the membership of the United Nations in the 30 years since its establishment, in order that the numerous small and medium-sized countries which currently constituted the vast majority of Member States could enjoy corresponding rights to speak and to make decisions in the main organs of the United Nations. . . . It could be seen that an increasing number of countries had joined the ranks of those advocating Charter review. The debate had once again convincingly demonstrated that the review and revision of the Charter was a manifestation of the general trend and of the aspirations of people.[11]

This statement clearly spelled out China's position regarding the charter review and reform question. While it was based on China's national interests and relations with other powers, it also communicated concern for how such a review might affect the interests of small- and medium-sized countries ("the majority of Member States") and how China's position reflected the "general trend and . . . the aspirations of people."

Practical Concerns Regarding Specific UN Organizational Reforms Since 2000

In June 2005, the Chinese government published a position paper describing specific guidelines for UN reforms in general and Security Council reforms in particular.[12] Rather than substantive legal changes, the guidelines were oriented toward practical issues such as development projects, poverty, security, rule of law, human rights, and democracy, with some statements addressing the idea of overall strengthening of the United Nations and its various organizations. Its suggested approach to reform emphasizes gradual change based on democratic consultations and a broad consensus on increasing the status and voting power of developing countries, which account for more than two-thirds of UN membership. In the 2005 position paper, China expressed an intention to defend the UN Constitution and its regulatory power. There was only one mention of a specific legal issue—Article 51, which addresses rules for the use of military force.

The June 2005 position paper can be compared with one published a month earlier by the "Group of Four" (Germany, Japan, India, and Brazil), which contained language suggesting that the UN Security Council had become anachronistic and no longer reflected actual global balances of power.[13] From the Chinese perspective, any Council expansion should be based on the interests of African countries rather than the Group of Four. Another reason for China's opposition was the inclusion of Japan, which China described as having more influence on the Security Council than it should only because of its financial contributions to the UN. According to the Chinese argument, Japan's influence should be tied to its current and past adherence to peace principles, and based on that standard, Japan was not yet qualified for permanent membership on the Security Council.[14] In contrast, Beijing took a passive approach to the potential admittance of Germany and Brazil to the Council, considering that neither country has ever supported China on issues such as human rights. Regarding India's application to join the Security Council, China expressed concerns about issues regarding the border between the two countries and India's views on questions involving Tibet.

For the Group of Four countries to achieve their Security Council membership goals, the number of permanent seats had to be increased, and while China had consistently expressed support for UN Security Council reforms, it rejected the idea of increasing the number of permanent seats without a strong regional consensus. This position was explained in detail in a 2004 article written by a former alternate representative to the UN Security Council, Miao-Fa Wu.[15] He explained that since the international situation had changed dramatically since the establishment of the UN, increasing the number of seats held by developing countries was required to maintain a proper representative balance. Thus, China believed that expanding the number of permanent Council seats should be discussed on a regional basis and that new permanent members should not be given veto power for reasons involving the history behind giving veto power to the original permanent Council members. This opinion was also expressed by Chinese scholar Jian-Fei Liu, who cited the significant contributions of the original five permanent members to winning the anti-fascist war.[16] On the question of veto power, Liu argued that giving it to too many countries would seriously reduce Security Council efficiency.[17]

When discussing principles to be followed when making Security Council reforms, Miao-Fa Wu[18] emphasized four points: a need to ensure that all Council members represent the realities of different world regions; the idea that developing countries formed the majority of UN members but were especially underrepresented on the Council; that becoming a permanent member symbolized a new status as a global or regional great power, therefore decisions to add new members demanded the utmost care; and veto power was such an important political question that it demanded thorough discussion in order to achieve a consensus.

Beijing's most recent position on Security Council reforms can be found in a statement presented by Chinese Ambassador Ma Zhaoxu at the First Meeting the 72nd General Assembly (2018), during which intergovernmental negotiations on Security Council reform were discussed:

> Reform of the Security Council is a complex and systemic project bearing on both the vital interests of Member States and the long-term development of the United Nations. It should be a democratic, consultative, transparent and inclusive process with a commitment to continuously build mutual trust and foster consensus. The five clusters of issues, namely, categories of membership, the question of veto, regional representation, the size and working methods of an enlarged

Council and the relationship between the Security Council and the General Assembly, form an integral whole with interconnectivity and interdependence. . . . In the seventy-plus years since its birth, the UN has witnessed its membership grow from 51 to 193. Most of the member states are developing countries and African states account for more than one fourth of the total UN membership. The rise of the developing countries as a group and the ascending power and influence of African states are prominent features of the international relations in the world we live now. The reform of the Security Council should reflect this reality by giving priority to the increase of the representation and voice of developing countries, particularly African counties, supporting African countries' efforts to rectify historical injustices, fully reflecting the will of regional countries in the decision making of the Security Council and enabling more small-and-medium-sized countries to play a bigger role in maintaining international peace and security.[19]

Conclusion

China's current general position on UN reforms stresses the following four points:

1   All reform proposals must clearly indicate a strengthening of UN authority and efficiency.
2   All reform proposals must prioritize and contribute to the representative weights of developing countries.
3   All final reform decisions must be based on a comprehensive consensus among UN members and cannot undermine UN solidarity.
4   China's position on any UN reform question will always emphasize general principles rather than concrete proposals.

The language in the last point fits with other characteristics of Chinese foreign policy and Beijing's approach to global governance in general: making broad and vaguely abstract statements without offering specific plans or agendas. China's reluctance to offer clear suggestions for UN reforms is not due to its dual status as a great power and permanent Security Council member with vested interests in the current UN system, but to a relationality dilemma involving the contradictory roles of a great power, a developing country, and a defender of the rights of all developing countries. These roles involve different types of relationality that cannot be adequately addressed within a multilateral framework such as the UN system. To successfully strike a balance, China will occasionally have to choose among them. Such decisions will not necessarily be based on power or interest concerns, but on how best to maintain a balance among different relationality types.

Notes

1 Suzanne Ogden, "China's Position on UN Charter Review," *Pacific Affairs*, 52(2) (1979), pp. 210–240.
2 趙磊，2005，〈中國對聯合國的外交政策：1949–1971—以人民日報涉及聯合國內容的文章為分析文本〉，《外交評論》，總第85期，頁61–67。
3 朱大偉，2009，〈聯合國安理會擴大改革的中國因素〉，《學習月刊》，總第245期，頁48–49。
4 Ogden, 1979, p. 213.
5 Egon Schwelb, 1966, "The 1963/1965 Amendments to the Charter of the United Nations: An Addendum," *The American Journal of International Law*, 60(2), footnote 3.
6 See also ibid., footnote 21, note by the Secretary-General and Explanatory Memorandum, September 16, 1965.
7 Emphasis original. General Assembly, Official Records: Twentieth Session, Supplement No. 14 (A/6014), No. 2101 (XX), "Amendment to Article 109 of the Charter of the United Nations," December 29, 1965, pp. 90–91.
8 Schwelb (1966), p. 377.
9 According to Chiu and Edwards, in a press conference held on September 29, 1965, Chinese Vice Premier Ch'en Yi unexpectedly advanced new conditions in addition to the expulsion of the Republic of China [Taiwan] representative in return for Communist China's participation in the UN. He argued, "The United Nations has long been controlled by the United States and has today become a place where two big powers, the United States and the Soviet Union, conduct political transactions." See Hungdah Chiu and Randle R. Edwards, "Communist China's Attitude toward the United Nations: A Legal Analysis," *American Journal of International Law*, 62 (1968), p. 37.
10 Ibid., pp. 21–25.
11 General Assembly—Thirtieth Section—Sixth Committee, 1578th Meeting, Tuesday, 2 December 1975, A/.6/SR.1578, p. 266.
12 Available at www.mfa.gov.cn/chn//pds/ziliao/tytj/t199083.htm, accessed August 10, 2018.
13 www.dw.com/en/security-council-reform-where-it-stands/a-1618479, accessed August 12, 2018.
14 劉文冬，2014，〈中國對安理會擴大的立場分析〉，《赤峰學院學報》，第35卷第10期，頁92–95。
15 吳妙發，2004，〈聯合國改革：一項重大的國際政治建設工程〉，《國際問題研究》，第5期，頁38–42.
16 劉建飛，2006，〈聯合國近年改革與中國外交〉，《國際關係學院學報》，第4期，頁41–46.
17 劉建飛，2006。
18 吳妙發，2004，頁40。
19 Published February 1, 2018. Available at www.china-un.org/eng/chinaandun/zzhgg/t1531601.htm, accessed August 13, 2018.

5   A Cold Peace in Cross-Strait Relations

Relationality Without Consensus

Introduction

The Nineteenth Chinese Communist Party Congress in 2017 raised many questions among academics about fragmented power within China's political system, leadership authority, and foreign policy-making. In previous studies of the country's political system and decision-making structure, Western observers have suggested that starting in the period following Deng Xiaoping's reforms and open policies, various internal and external challenges have resulted in a transition from a centralized totalitarian structure to a fragmented system consisting of various interest groups inside and outside the Party and state bureaucracies. Even the Party-state system's traditional reliance on authoritarian decision-making appeared to be gradually changing to a more collective process. However, the approach to governance approved by the Nineteenth Party Congress challenged many assumptions due to Xi Jinping's clear consolidation of personal power and the establishment of a "strongman" image. In this chapter, I will suggest that the impacts of reforms enacted by the Congress, plus Xi's strong control over foreign policy decisions and international behaviors, are the primary reasons for the increasingly negative relationship between China and Taiwan. Specifically, Xi's party-state structural reforms have made any consensus between China and Taiwan impossible due to contradictory relationalities embedded in cross-Strait relations: Xi aggressively presents himself as an authoritarian leader, while Taiwan continues to project a strongly democratic image. These contrasting types of relationality emphasize the fundamental differences that exist between the state and society, between political leaders and their citizens, and specifically between each of the two countries and the rest of the world.

Rising Nationalism in China

In its December 2016 issue, *Foreign Affairs* published an article entitled "How Democracies Fall Apart: Why Populism Is a Pathway to Autocracy."

DOI: 10.4324/9780429486616-5

It addressed a phenomenon that emerged following the US subprime mortgage crisis in 2008: a growing populism within democracies based on their citizens' growing unease with globalization, with immigration policies perceived as blurring national boundaries, and with weakened domestic employment protections. The best-known examples of this phenomenon include the Scottish movement to leave the United Kingdom, Brexit, and Donald Trump's unexpected electoral victory. None of these events were correctly predicted by existing theoretical approaches.

There appeared to be growing confidence in Western democracy prior to the 2008 economic crisis,[1] with calls to reassess the role of the state in a new age of global governance,[2] and with new theoretical approaches such as neoliberal institutionalism and constructivism, both suggesting the potential for new types of cooperation among nation-states and between individuals.[3] The confidence was false, and the period instead focused on the shortcomings of globalization, questions about the functions of global governance institutions such as the WTO, IMF and World Bank, and concerns about nationalism, independence versus interdependence, autonomy, and sovereignty.

Against this backdrop, the People's Republic of China energetically pursued its goals while democratic governments were forced to deal with their various populist movements. Over the past ten years, it has expressed limited support for the established liberal-democratic model of global governance, while surpassing Japan to become the world's second largest economy.[4] China's current status as an economic powerhouse (if not a superpower) can be interpreted as one result of its long-term efforts to integrate into the world's liberal markets and international society following Deng Xiaoping's push for reforms and open policies, with the country gradually changing its status as a recipient of assistance from the established Western-led liberal system[5] to a supporter and defender of that system. Thus, we find China making alliances with European countries to tackle climate change by reaffirming the funding commitments of the Paris agreement and promising to enact strong domestic policies concerning greenhouse gas reduction and energy efficiency.[6] Now that Syria and Nicaragua have signed the Paris climate accord, the United States is the only country on the planet that has yet to sign. Then in October 2017, the United States announced its withdrawal from the United Nations Educational, Scientific and Cultural Organization (UNESCO).[7] The assistant director-general for education at UNESCO, Qian Tang, is Chinese, and it is generally believed that he wants to become the head of the entire agency. In a recent interview, he described China as "want[ing] to fulfill its global responsibility and contribute to peace and development at a global level."[8] These and many other examples show that as democratic countries such as the United States move away from globalization and toward conservative nationalism, an authoritative Chinese regime is participating in international organizations and voicing support for their institutional values.

China has increasingly perceived a need to do things outside of existing international organizations, with the two best-known examples being the One Belt, One Road project, and the Asian Infrastructure Investment Bank. Apparently at one time, the Chinese government considered asking for approval or even financial support for these projects from established financial institutions such as the World Bank and IMF, but after years of objections from other nations, mostly the United States, Beijing decided to follow Mao Zedong's strategy of *lingqi luzao* (literally "building a new stove") by creating its own institutions.[9] Militarily, China is projecting a more assertive regional posture toward protecting "core interests" in maritime disputes in the East China Sea and South China Sea,[10] building new military facilities on disputed islands in the latter to solidify its claims. In the words of the Asia Maritime Transparency Initiative (part of the Center for Strategic and International Studies in Washington, DC), China is "militarizing the region."[11] In July 2016, an international tribunal in The Hague rebuked China's claims of historical rights over most of the South China Sea and deemed its construction of artificial islands as illegal. China's response was to ignore the decision as "invalid" and having "no binding force."[12]

China is engaging in international debates over multiple political and domestic issues. For example, Beijing claims that it is executing the most thorough and far-reaching anti-corruption campaign since Mao Zedong.[13] However, many Western observers have described the shortcomings of the Chinese Communist Party and Xi Jinping in terms of abusing power in the name of the campaign, including human rights and civil rights violations and efforts to purge the Party of all voices that are not in lockstep with Xi's political interests and ambitions. The Western media has described the Central Commission for Discipline Inspection (the name of the lead anti-corruption campaign institution) as a secretive agency that Xi has mostly used to consolidate his power and weaken rival factions within the Party.[14] The politicized Commission operates outside the country's legal system, and from the perspective of Western China watchers, its main purpose is to create fear rather than pursue injustices.[15]

China regularly presents two images on the international stage. It plays a self-written role as a responsible great power while projecting an image of moving from pure participant status to that of a supporter or defender of the established international political and economic order, one still dominated by the United States and other Western countries, at least for the time being. Thus, Chinese foreign policy is increasingly determined by a mix of development-centered domestic politics and an external environment requiring significant support from the international community.[16] At the same time, China is taking more proactive and assertive actions in terms of large-scale economic projects such as the Belt and Road Initiative, military modernization, and political reforms—all tightly controlled by the Chinese Communist Party (CCP). In this sense, the country's foreign policy is being used in the service of domestic goals that support the needs of the Party, the Chinese leadership, and the Chinese nation. If these three areas are analyzed as central elements of a Chinese governance model, it is possible to identify measures of foreign policy success. For some analysts, the three-part model reflects a growing Chinese nationalism—in an article published in *The China Review* entitled "Nationalism and Chinese Foreign Policy," Tianbiao Zhu warns about the "danger of the means contradicting the goal of nationalism."[17] According to Zhu, China's efforts to defend its national or cultural identity is bound to be increasingly subject to external challenges if not outright attacks from the outside world.

Xi's Power Consolidation

To assess the impacts of Xi Jinping's internal control monopoly and personal power consolidation on Chinese foreign policy, it is important to discuss how China balances its perceived needs for international responsibility and domestic development, including the pursuit of nationalist goals. There is a large English-language literature on Chinese politics that describes its foreign policy-making processes in terms of an ideal model that resists the dominance of a single individual on major policy questions, while encouraging a system that is more open, professional, decentralized, and willing to deal with fragmentation.[18] Many scholars have described Chinese foreign policy decisions as being made by a "collective leadership" in which the CCP General Secretary is considered "first among equals" within a ministerial cabinet-style structure.[19] However, some critics note that even if a sense of professionalism did emerge in bureaucratic departments or local governments, it is questionable whether it would ever become a true substitute for centralized control over policy-making. Taiwanese scholar Chien-min Chao believes that regardless of whether the country's leadership is dominated by a strong single individual or multiple actors, all policy decisions must be made on a situation- or issue-dependent basis.[20]

When analyzing the Chinese political apparatus from the 1990s to date, some Western scholars such as David Lampton believe that Beijing's foreign policy-making process (at least pre-Xi) reveals major problems resulting from a fragmented and decentralized Chinese bureaucratic structure, which initially made it difficult for both central and local governments to implement Xi's decisions. Lampton uses the country's National Security

Commission as an example of how long-term disagreements between external and internal security concerns, or between military and diplomatic bureaucracies, encouraged Xi to find solutions for practical coordination issues (especially domestic governance issues) when consolidating his personal power.[21] Others have cited Lampton's argument when discussing Xi's numerous self-appointed titles: Chairman of the Central Military Commission, Leader of the Central Leading Group for Foreign Affairs, Leader of the Central Leading Group for Taiwan Affairs, Leader of the Central Leading Group for Comprehensively Deepening Reforms, Chairman of the Central National Security Commission, and Leader of the Central Leading Group for Internet Security and Information, among others.[22] In the past, power in China deemphasized institutions—Deng Xiaoping quit all of his formal positions in 1989—but still retained all of his power. Apparently, Xi believes that formal titles are required to justify his authority or to recover fragmented influence distributed over multiple divisions and bureaucratic units.

Concepts such as "checks and balances" and "separation of powers" that are considered core values in the United States and democracies such as Taiwan have neither history nor currency in China.[23] Thus, when China watchers try to make sense of current political reforms or impacts from the 19th Party Congress—especially in terms of who is serving on the Politburo's Standing Committee—they frequently express frustration as well as pessimism about China's future. Xi Jinping has amassed enormous power since 2013, and there is no obvious successor in sight, feeding speculation that he has no plans to relinquish power after the usual five- or ten-year leadership cycle.[24] This raises all kinds of concerns in the West about "steps backwards" and a return to a Mao-like dictatorship, concerns leading China watchers to once again reexamine fundamental differences in political values and norms between China and the West. According to Rex Tillerson, former chairman and chief executive officer of ExxonMobil who served as US Secretary of State for one year during the Trump administration, the United States can never forge the same type of relationship with China as it has with democratic countries.[25] This raises two important questions: How might a Chinese governance model with a strongman at the center ultimately challenge the Western model? And how is the West supposed to react when a non-Western type of governance system controls the world's second largest economy? For countries in various stages of development, China offers proof that it is unnecessary to adhere to a Western liberal governance model in order to achieve economic success or political stability.

Other challenges for those wanting to assess the impacts of Xi's domestic and Party reforms on Chinese foreign policy include assumptions that power concentrated in a single central leadership will result in an arbitrary decision-making process marked by acts of assertiveness that are increasingly confrontational. In Xi's report to the 19th Party Congress, there is evidence of both proactive/assertive and humanitarian-oriented foreign policy approaches and positions. The latter includes Chinese intentions to create a new type of international relations and the establishment of what Xi calls "a community of common destiny with mankind."[26] Details are lacking—mostly vague statements about working with all countries to establish a long-lasting peace based on the principles of general security and common prosperity, ridding the world of Cold War thinking and power politics, and insisting on dialogue to resolve disputes and reconcile divisions. At the same time, Xi is working hard to create a powerful military force with international reach and has regularly emphasized the essential participation of the CCP in China's rise. According to Xi, it is the Party's obligation to ensure and protect the pursuit of happiness for all Chinese, therefore consolidating his power will likely exert stronger impacts on domestic governance than on foreign policy concerns. If this interpretation is correct, Xi's tightening of party control and periodic announcements of anti-corruption campaigns will be used to retain domestic support,[27] with significant impacts on party members and intellectuals, but not on the daily lives of most Chinese. In other words, if Xi's legitimacy, as well as that of the CCP, is based on current political reforms within the Party, his consolidation of power may be viewed by the Chinese populace as a step in establishing and maintaining legitimacy—an acceptable idea for most Chinese.

When considering the impacts of Xi's power consolidation on Beijing's foreign policy edicts and behaviors, it is incorrect to only expect more policy coordination, power concentration, or increased assertiveness. What actually occurs will depend on which issues are attracting Xi's attention at any given moment. For example, on November 30, 2016, the UN Security Council imposed sanctions aimed at cutting North Korea's largest export product, coal, by 60%.[28] The Chinese government initially supported the sanctions, but later claimed that a lack of coordination among the PRC Ministry of Commerce, Ministry of Foreign Affairs, and General Customs Administration allowed North Korean coal exports to exceed the quota stipulated by UN Security Council Resolution 2321 between December 1 and 15,[29] when the Ministry of Commerce finally announced a coal import ban. One may interpret the delay either as a buffer period prior to implementing a specific policy, or as the very first time for the Chinese government to vote in favor of sanctions aimed at North Korea.

Another example is the standoff that took place at the Doklam border station between China and India from June 18 to August 28, 2017, when Indian and Chinese troops confronted each other over a road construction project. Some analysts describe China's assertive posture toward both Bhutan and

India as fitting with its general shift toward more forceful behavior on international and regional stages.[30] Initially, there was agreement involving the construction or repair of 30 roads in the area, an agreement that normally would require central government approval, and therefore presumably known by President Xi. However, it is also possible that Xi did not believe that a simple case of road construction might reignite a Sino-India border conflict. As expected, the Chinese Ministry of Foreign Affairs immediately criticized India's "illegal" behavior in violation of Chinese territorial sovereignty. One important question is whether Chinese troops were performing road construction without keeping the Ministry of Foreign Affairs fully informed, and if so, why not. It is one possible explanation for why the Ministry responded in such strong terms, thus putting China in a position that might have required unilateral compromises. It took more than two months for the two sides to resolve the crisis via diplomatic channels.[31]

Conclusion

Due to the multilateral relationality perspective that has long been favored in Western countries, the current international political order is based on rules and practices requiring self-restraint on the part of state actors. Since self-restraint reveals an actor's willingness to temporarily sacrifice its own interests for the sake of maintaining relationships with others according to multilateral rules, those actors might proclaim exceptionalism when certain rules are not to their liking. Under Xi Jinping's leadership, Beijing seems to be backing away from the foreign policy principle that it has abided by for decades: *tao guang yang hui* ("hide one's ability and bide one's time")—in other words, self-restraint. China's increasingly assertive foreign policy behaviors signal a movement away from an established world order that is based on multilateral relationality, a world order that Taiwan is doing everything in its power to join. However, a gap exists between the Chinese leadership and the country's foreign policy behaviors—even though Xi has consolidated considerable power, he cannot effectively control all developments in foreign affairs. This gap will likely get smaller if domestic nationalism intensifies, or if Xi decides to disregard constraints imposed by an earlier, more conventional collective leadership doctrine. In both cases, China will move in a polar-opposite direction from the democratic practices and Western style of multilateralism currently found in Taiwan.

Notes

1 Francis Fukuyama, *The End of History and the Last Man* (New York: Free Press, 1992).

2 James N. Rosenau and Ernst Otto Czempiel, *Governance without Government: Order and Change in World Politics* (Cambridge: Cambridge University Press, 1992).

3 Robert O. Keohane and Helen V. Milner, *Internationalization and Domestic Politics* (Cambridge: Cambridge University Press, 1996); Judith Goldstein, *Ideas, Interests, and American Trade Politics* (Ithaca: Cornell University Press, 1993); Alexander Wendt, *Social Theory of International Politics* (Cambridge, UK: Cambridge University Press, 1999).

4 www.nytimes.com/2010/08/16/business/global/16yuan.html?pagewanted=all, accessed October 24, 2017.

5 John Ikenberry, "The Rise of China and the Future of the West: Can the Liberal System Survive?" *Foreign Affairs*, 87(1) (January/February 2008), pp. 1–23.

6 www.theguardian.com/environment/2017/may/31/china-eu-climate-lead-paris-agreement, accessed October 24, 2017.

7 www.unesco.org/archives/multimedia/?pg=33&s=films_details&id=198, accessed October 24, 2017.

8 http://foreignpolicy.com/2017/10/06/as-u-s-retreats-from-world-organizations-china-steps-in-the-fill-the-void/#, accessed October 24, 2017.

9 Chunjuan Nancy Wei, "New Chinese Banks: Right out of Mao's Playbook?" *The Diplomat*, March 20, 2015, available at https://thediplomat.com/2015/03/new-chinese-banks-right-out-of-maos-playbook/, accessed October 24, 2017.

10 According to a report released by the US-China Economic and Security Review Commission, it wasn't until 2009 that China publicly defined its core interests. See Caitlin Campbell, Ethan Meick, Kimberly Hsu, and Craig Murray, "China's 'Core Interests' and the East China Sea," US-China Economic and Security Review Commission Staff Research Backgrounder, May 10, 2013, available at www.uscc.gov/sites/default/files/Research/China's%20Core%20Interests%20and%20the%20East%20China%20Sea.pdf, accessed October 24, 2017. For the South China Sea issue, see Toshi Yoshihara and James R. Holmes, "Can China Defend a 'Core Interest' in the South China Sea?" *The Washington Quarterly* (Spring 2011), pp. 45–59.

11 https://amti.csis.org/

12 Jane Perlez, "Tribunal Rejects Beijing's Claims in South China Sea," *The New York Times*, July 12, 2016, available at www.nytimes.com/2016/07/13/world/asia/south-china-sea-hague-ruling-philippines.html, accessed October 24, 2017.

13 Hudson Lockett, "China Anti-corruption Campaign Backfires," *Financial Times*, October 10, 2016, available at www.ft.com/content/02f712b4-8ab8-11e6-8aa5-f79f5696c731, accessed October 24, 2017.

14 William Wan, "Secretive Agency Leads Most Intense Anti-Corruption Effort in Modern Chinese History," *The Washington Post*, July 2, 2014, available at www.washingtonpost.com/world/asia_pacific/secretive-agency-leads-most-intense-anti-corruption-effort-in-modern-chinese-history/2014/07/02/48aff932-cf68-11e3-937f-d3026234b51c_story.html?utm_term=.3e01e5a7ddeb, accessed October 24, 2017.

15 Reuters Staff, "Illegal Detention and Torture underpin China's Corruption Crackdown: Human Rights Watch Report," *Reuters*, December 6, 2016, available at www.reuters.com/article/us-china-rights/illegal-detention-and-torture-underpin-chinas-corruption-crackdown-human-rights-watch-report-idUSKBN13V0LQ, accessed October 24, 2017.

16 This implies a shift in emphasis in Chinese foreign policy from the popular view held in the 1990s as an extension of China's domestic politics. See, for example, "Qian Qichen on the World Situation," *Beijing Review*, 33(3) (1990), pp. 16–18.

17 Tianbiao Zhu, "Nationalism and Chinese Foreign Policy," *The China Review*, 1(1) (Fall 2001), p. 5.

18 See, for example, Doak A. Barnett, *The Making of Foreign Policy in China: Structure and Process* (Boulder, CO: Westview Press, 1985); Kenneth G. Lieberthal and Michel Oksenberg, *Policy Making in China: Leaders, Structures, and Process* (Princeton, NJ: Princeton University Press, 1988); Carol Lee Hamrin and Zhao Suisheng, *Decision-making in Deng's China: Perspective from Insiders* (Armonk, NY: Sharpe, 1995); David M. Lampton, ed., *The Making of Chinese Foreign and Security Policy in the Era of Reform* (Stanford, CA: Stanford University Press, 2001).

19 Yu-shan Wu, "Jiang and After: Technocratic Rule, Generational Replacement and Mentor Politics," in Yun-hab Chu, Zhicheng Luo, and Ramon Hawley Myers, eds., *The New Chinese Leadership: Challenges and Opportunities after the 16th Party Congress* (Cambridge: Cambridge University Press, 2004), p. 65.

20 Chien-min Chao, *Chinese Policy Making: Leadership, Structure, Mechanism and Process* (Taipei: Wunan Publisher, 2014).

21 David M. Lampton, "Xi Jinping and the National Security Commission: Policy Coordination and Political Power," in Shusheng Zhao, ed., *The Making of China's Foreign Policy in the 21st Century* (New York: Routledge, 2016).

22 Zheping Huang, "China's President Xi Jinping Now Has a Dozen Titles, and Counting," *QUARTZ*, January 23, 2017, available at https://qz.com/892208/chinas-president-xi-jinping-now-has-a-dozen-titles-and-counting/, accessed October 29, 2017.

23 According to the Xinhua News Agency (the official media outlet for the Chinese government), Wang Qishan, a key figure in Xi Jinping's anti-corruption campaign, once said that "there is no such thing as the separation of powers between the party and the government." See Jiangtao Shi, " 'No Separation of Powers': China's Top Graft-Buster Seeks Tighter Party Grip on Government," *South China Morning Post*, March 6, 2017, available at www.scmp.com/news/china/policies-politics/article/2076501/no-separation-powers-chinas-top-graft-buster-seeks, accessed November 5, 2017. According to a comment made by scholar Zuo-lai Wu during a visit to the US, a secret "document No. 9" contains seven rules controlling forbidden acts; one of them is that the media, university scholars, and students cannot talk about separation of powers, democratic constitutions, civil society, or universal values. See Zuo-lai Wu, "Review China: Will Xi Jinping Have Another Big Action?" *BBC News* (Chinese version), November 4, 2013, available at www.bbc.com/zhongwen/trad/focus_on_china/2013/11/131104_cr_xilireform_bywuzuolai, accessed November 5.

24 Chris Buckley, "Xi Jinping Unveils China's New Leaders but No Clear Successor," *The New York Times*, October 24, 2017, available at www.nytimes.com/2017/10/24/world/asia/xi-jinping-china.html, accessed November 5, 2017.

25 Rex Tillerson, "Defining Our Relationship with India for the Next Century: An Address by US Secretary of State Rex Tillerson," Center for Strategic & International Studies, October 18, 2017, available at www.csis.org/analysis/defining-our-relationship-india-next-century-address-us-secretary-state-rex-tillerson, accessed November 2, 2017.

26 For the full text, see http://news.sina.com.cn/o/2017-10-18/doc-ifymyyxw35 16456.shtml, accessed November 2, 2017.

27 Wen-bin Liu and Jen-chih Cheng, "An Analysis of Xi Jinping's Anti-Corruption Campaign from the Perspective of Authoritarianism with Chinese Style," *Prospect & Exploration*, 12(4) (April 2014), pp. 83–110.

28 Somini Sengupta and Jane Perlez, "UN Stiffens Sanctions on North Korea, Trying to Slow Its Nuclear March," *The New York Times*, November 30, 2016, available at www.nytimes.com/2016/11/30/world/asia/north-korea-un-sanctions.html, accessed November 5, 2017.

29 Yun Sun, "The Myth of China's Coal Imports from North Korea," 38 North (a project of the US-Korea Institute at Johns Hopkins University School of Advanced International Studies), April 5, 2017, available at www.38north.org/2017/04/ysun040517/, accessed November 5, 2017.

30 Dan Southerland, "Bhutan in a Bind Amid Himalayan Standoff Between China and India," *Radio Free Asia*, August 18, 2017, available at www.rfa.org/english/commentaries/india-china-08182017175038.html, accessed November 5, 2017.

31 James Griffiths, "India, China Agree to 'Expeditious Disengagement' of Doklam Border Dispute," CNN News, August 29, 2017, available at http://edition.cnn.com/2017/08/28/asia/india-china-brics-doklam/index.html, accessed November 5, 2017.

6 Taiwan-Related Images in *Time* and *Newsweek*

Introduction

This chapter uses visual images to show how Taiwan was portrayed in photographs and cartoons published in the Asian editions of two mass-circulation American news magazines over a 29-year period. Both *Time* and *Newsweek* contain many examples of ways that American news periodicals in general emphasize cultural values such as democracy and human rights when discussing Taiwan. The American media has assigned roles to Taiwan as an independent country, a sovereign state, a democratic country, and a weak state under continuous threat from a rising communist China. In their articles and editorial cartoons on the topic of dealing with China's rising power and its perceived threat to both Taiwan and the United States, these two magazines in particular have repeatedly cited reasons for positioning democratic Taiwan in opposition to communist China. They describe the United States and Taiwan as "like-minded countries" with "shared values." The degree to which specific periodicals influence the thinking of the American public and its political leaders cannot be specifically measured, but Congress has repeatedly shown support for Taiwan in the form of bills encouraging official diplomatic exchanges and major arms sales, both of which automatically receive the harshest possible criticisms from the Chinese leadership.

The period between 1990 and 2018 was selected for this analysis because it allows for the inclusion of American views toward Taiwan at the end of the Cold War.[1] The motivation for this chapter is to show how two established American newsmagazines disseminated carefully crafted images of Taiwan as a pro-American, pro-democracy, anti-communist Chinese state. Admittedly, there are multiple ways to explore a theme as broad as "current US perspectives on Taiwan," depending on how those perspectives are defined. Do they refer to the general opinions of the American public? Or by official policy statements from the US government, the individual or

DOI: 10.4324/9780429486616-6

collective views of American politicians, or the evaluations of American or other Western scholars? None of these can be considered as fully representative, but for the purposes of this chapter, I will specifically focus on Taiwan-related views and perspectives emphasized by *Time* and *Newsweek* and then discuss my observations in terms of American public opinion, government statements, and scholarly evaluations.

The chosen method for this review is based on the approach used by David Dimitri Perlmutter in his *Visual Images and Foreign Policy: Picturing China in The American Press, 1949–1989* (1996).[2] However, an important difference should be noted in terms of interpretation: the method used in this chapter entails determining how the combination of picture clusters and report analyses present consistent associations of Taiwan with values frequently described as "American" and how they reflect ideologies or worldviews consistently promoted by the US government. The ideas presented in this chapter are based on the assumption that the American media—even in the form of editions aimed specifically at readers living in other countries—plays a major role in shaping public opinion about international affairs, both positive and negative. It is also assumed that the power of American media has shaped the way that Taiwanese view their own country—a shared identity constructed by institutions and political entities in Taiwan and the United States. The data presented in this chapter indicate that the editorial slants of the two news magazines regarding Taiwan were far from neutral during the study period. It even appears that occasional editorial criticism of America's Taiwan policy—or, more accurately, its China policy—has benefited Taiwan.

This chapter consists of two parts. The first will present results from my investigation of how *Time* and *Newsweek* regularly depicted Taiwan between 1990 and 2018, as measured in terms of Taiwan-related images (photos and cartoons), their prominence, and the amount of page space given to them. The second part will examine these same measures in 1996 and 2000—two peak years for coverage of Taiwan-related stories in the two magazines.

Portrayals of Taiwan

The results presented in this chapter are from a page-by-page inspection of *Time* and *Newsweek* issues published between January 1, 1990, and December 31, 2018. All images of Taiwan were identified and coded in terms of format: photograph, chart, graph, or cartoon. Magazine articles were examined in the contexts of these images, which were measured in terms of focus, frequency of appearance per year, prominence, and surface area (page space).

Focus

This measure indicates the total number of Taiwan-related images appearing on the pages of *Time* or *Newsweek* during the study period. The results shown in Table 6.1 need to be interpreted carefully—in several cases, the word "Taiwan" appeared in a caption or headline, but the image and related story cannot be considered Taiwan-focused. One example is the January 8, 1990, *Time* cover image of a famous Taiwanese singer-songwriter with the words "A controversial balladeer, not a *baotu*:[3] Hou Dejian in Beijing." The story is not about Taiwan, but about the way that Mainland Chinese authorities reacted to Hou's participation in the 1989 protests at Tiananmen Square. In contrast, the April 2, 1990, *Time* cover image is clearly about Taiwan's political reforms: a photo of thousands of protesting Taiwanese accompanied by the caption "Taiwan's 'Tiananmen: student demonstrations at the Chiang Kai-shek Memorial.'" Results for all photos clearly identified as being about Taiwan or a Taiwan-related topic are displayed in Table 6.2. The data indicate that *Newsweek* published an average of 2.3 more pictures per year than *Time* between 1990 and 2018.

Frequency

Table 6.3 and Figures 6.1 and 6.2 present results for the yearly frequencies of Taiwan-focused images published in the two magazines, individually and combined, between 1990 and 2018.

Table 6.1 Taiwan-related images in *Time* and *Newsweek* between 1990 and 2018

Publication	Total Number of Images	Percentage of All Images Published in the Two Periodicals
Time	235	45
Newsweek	283	55
Total	518	100

Table 6.2 Taiwan-focused images published in *Time* and *Newsweek* between 1990 and 2018

Publication	Number of Taiwan-Focused Images	Percentage of All Taiwan-Focused Images in the Two Magazines
Time	171	44
Newsweek	218	56
Total	389	100

Table 6.3 Taiwan-related images appearing in *Time* or *Newsweek* per year between 1990 and 2018

Year	Time Frequency	Time Percentage	Newsweek Frequency	Newsweek Percentage	Time + Newsweek Frequency	Time + Newsweek Percentage
1990	9	5.3	13	6.0	22	5.7
1991	3	1.8	18	8.3	21	5.4
1992	2	1.2	12	5.5	14	3.6
1993	3	1.8	11	5.0	14	3.6
1994	1	0.6	17	7.8	18	4.7
1995	17	9.9	9	4.1	26	6.7
1996	27	15.8	29	13.3	56	14.5
1997	8	4.7	4	1.8	12	3.1
1998	3	1.8	7	3.2	10	2.6
1999	14	8.2	8	3.7	22	5.7
2000	27	15.8	31	14.2	58	15.0
2001	6	3.5	8	3.7	14	3.6
2002	3	1.8	7	3.2	10	2.6
2003	1	0.6	0	0.0	1	0.3
2004	7	4.1	17	7.8	24	6.2
2005	4	2.3	7	3.2	11	2.8
2006	5	2.9	6	2.8	11	2.8
2007	2	1.2	0	0.0	2	0.5
2008	7	4.1	6	2.8	13	3.4
2009	2	1.2	0	0.0	2	0.5
2010	0	0.0	0	0.0	0	0.0
2011	0	0.0	0	0.0	0	0.0
2012	3	1.8	0	0.0	3	0.8
2013	0	0.0	0	0.0	0	0.0
2014	3	1.8	NA	NA	NA	NA
2015	8	4.7	2	0.9	10	2.6
2016	3	1.8	2	0.9	5	1.3
2017	1	0.6	3	1.4	4	1.0
2018	2	1.2	1	0.5	3	0.8
Total	171	100	218	100	386	100
Mean	5.9		7.8		13.8	

Differences between *Time* and *Newsweek* can be interpreted in terms of individual frequencies (Table 6.4). The data show that *Newsweek* published more Taiwan-associated images than *Time* in 14 of the 29 years reviewed, fewer than *Time* in 11, and the same in 4. This difference in images is considered important because on a yearly average, *Newsweek* devoted twice as many pages as *Time* to stories about Taiwan (6.1 versus 3.2), indicating dominant coverage in *Newsweek* (Table 6.4).

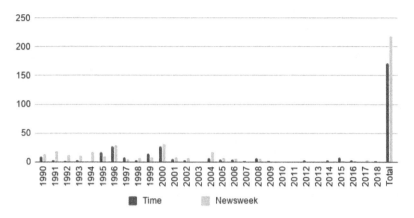

Figure 6.1 Taiwan-related images appearing in *Time* or *Newsweek* per year between 1990 and 2018.

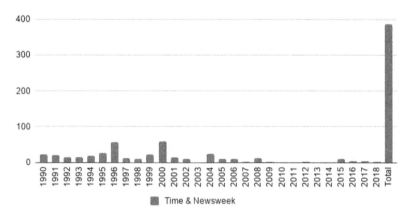

Figure 6.2 Taiwan-related images appearing in *Time* and *Newsweek* combined per year between 1990 and 2018.

Table 6.5 presents data showing when the frequency of published sto-ries about Taiwan was more (+) or less (−) than 20% of the total mean frequency[4] for that publication during the designated year ("=" indicates the same frequency or similar frequencies). The results indicate equal or near-equal frequencies for 12 of the 28 years reviewed. In three of those

Table 6.4 Differences in Taiwan-related image frequencies in *Time* and *Newsweek*

Year	Time *(+)*	Newsweek *(+)*
1990	–	+4
1991	–	+15
1992	–	+10
1993	–	+8
1994	–	+16
1995	+8	–
1996	–	+2
1997	+4	–
1998	–	+4
1999	+6	–
2000	–	+4
2001	–	+2
2002	–	+4
2003	+1	–
2004	–	+10
2005	–	+3
2006	–	+1
2007	+2	–
2008	+1	–
2009	+2	–
2010	–	–
2011	–	–
2012	+3	–
2013	–	–
2014	NA	NA
2015	+6	–
2016	+1	–
2017	–	+2
2018	+1	–
Total	171	218
Number of years publishing more images/ average number of images per year	11/3.2	14/6.1

years (1990, 1996, and 2000), the matching frequencies were higher than 20% of the total mean frequency. In 1990, the Taiwanese economy was starting a long period of growth and political reform following the end of the Cold War. In 1996, Lee Teng-hui became the first democratically elected president in 5,000 years of Chinese history, and the region suffered from the effects of what is today known as the Taiwan Strait Missile Crisis. In 2000, the pro-Taiwan independent candidate Chen Shui-bian won the presidential election, marking the end of 50 years of governance by the KMT party.

Table 6.5 High and low Taiwan-related image frequency years for *Time* and *Newsweek* individually

Year	Time *(+)*	Newsweek *(+)*
1990	+	+
1991	−	+
1992	−	+
1993	−	+
1994	−	+
1995	+	=
1996	+	+
1997	+	−
1998	−	=
1999	+	=
2000	+	+
2001	=	=
2002	+	=
2003	−	−
2004	=	+
2005	−	=
2006	−	−
2007	−	−
2008	=	−
2009	−	−
2010	−	−
2011	−	−
2012	−	−
2013	−	−
2014	−	NA
2015	+	−
2016	−	−
2017	−	−
2018	−	−
Total	171	218
Mean	5.9	7.8
Total low years	18	14
Total number of average years	3	6
Total number of high years	8	8
Total number of matching low years	11	11
Total number of matching average years	1	1
Total number of matching high years	3	3
Total number of matching years	15	15

Prominence

This measure refers to the visibility of Taiwan-related images in the two magazines, a simple example being the appearance of a Taiwan-focused photo on the cover, which is considered as having greater prominence than a photo on an interior page. For the purposes of this book, "cover photo" (or "cover image") is defined as one-half or more of an issue's front page. Table 6.6 presents results for the average yearly numbers of cover photos in the two magazines; they show that *Newsweek* gave more prominence than *Time* to Taiwan-related images. Table 6.7 shows data for a comparison of Taiwan-related cover stories by year; the same data is displayed visually in Figure 6.3. As shown, Taiwan-related stories were given greatest prominence in 1996 and 2000.

Space

The final measure indicates the amount of space devoted to images. For both *Time* and *Newsweek*, one page is 20.5 cm by 27.5 cm in size—564 square centimeters, 1,128 for two pages, 282 for a half-page. Table 6.8 presents data for the amount of space dedicated to Taiwan-related images in *Time*, and Table 6.9 presents the same information for *Newsweek*. The

Table 6.6 Taiwan image prominence in *Time* and *Newsweek*, 1990–2018

Publication	Average Yearly Frequency of Taiwan Cover Stories	Percentage of Taiwan Cover Stories Between the Two Magazines	Taiwan Cover Images as Percentage of Total Taiwan-Focused Images in the Two Magazines
Time	6	37.5	3.5
Newsweek	10	62.5	4.6
Total	16	100.0	8.1

Table 6.7: Taiwan Image Prominence between Publications by Year

Year	Time Covers	Newsweek Covers	Time & Newsweek Covers
1990	0	0	0
1991	0	1	1
1992	0	0	0
1993	0	0	0
1994	0	1	1
1995	1	0	1
1996	2	2	4
1997	0	0	0
1998	0	0	0
1999	0	0	0
2000	1	3	4
2001	1	0	1

(Continued)

Year	Time Covers	Newsweek Covers	Time & Newsweek Covers
2002	0	2	2
2003	0	0	0
2004	0	1	1
2005	0	0	0
2006	0	0	0
2007	0	0	0
2008	0	0	0
2009	0	0	0
2010	0	0	0
2011	0	0	0
2012	0	0	0
2013	0	0	0
2014	0	0	0
2015	1	0	1
2016	0	0	0
2017	0	0	0
2018	0	0	0
Total	6	10	16

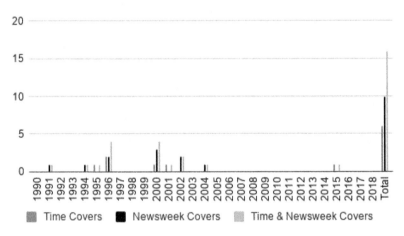

Figure 6.3 Taiwan image prominence by year for *Time* and *Newsweek*, 1990–2018.

tables clearly show that *Newsweek* devoted more space than *Time* to images associated with Taiwan news stories or analyses: 35,706 versus 26,559 square centimeters (57% versus 43% of the total space for each

Table 6.8 Surface area given to Taiwan-related images in *Time*

Image Size	Number	Percentage of All Images	Surface Area (sq. cm)	Percentage of All Surface Area
2 pages	8	4.7	9,024	24.9
1 page	15	8.8	8,460	23.4
Half-page	28	16.4	7,896	21.8
Quarter-page	42	24.6	5,922	16.4
One-ninth page & smaller	78	45.6	4,914	13.6
Total	171	≈100	36,216	≈100

Table 6.9 Surface area given to Taiwan-related images in *Newsweek*

Image Size	Frequency	Percent	Surface Area (sq. cm)	Percent of All Surface Area (sq. cm)
2 pages	4	1.8	4,512	11.3
1 page	20	9.2	11,280	28.2
Half-page	33	15.1	9,306	23.7
Quarter-page	61	27.9	8,601	21.5
One-ninth page or smaller	100	45.9	6,300	15.7
Total	218	≈100	39,999	≈100

magazine). However, *Time* published more images taking up one full page or parts of two pages compared to *Newsweek*; both had roughly the same number of images that were one-quarter page or smaller. Table 6.10 presents surface area data for individual years between 1990 and 2018; it shows an average yearly surface area of 1,488 square centimeters for *Newsweek* compared to 1,107 for *Time*.

Overall Comparison

A summary of Taiwan-related images appearing in the two magazines is presented in Table 6.11. As shown, *Newsweek* scored higher (5–25%) in all categories, with the largest difference in cover page images. Table 6.12 shows which magazine had more images during individual years. According to this data, peak coverage for both magazines occurred in the same years, 1996 and 2000. The next highest levels of peak appearances of Taiwan-related images occurred in 1991 and 1994 for *Newsweek* and 1995 for *Time*.

Table 6.10 Surface area given to Taiwan-related images in *Time* and *Newsweek* by year

Year	Time (sq. cm)	Time (%)	Newsweek (sq. cm)	Newsweek (%)	Total (sq. cm)	Total (%)
1990	723	2.0	1,209	3.0	1,932	2.6
1991	189	0.5	1,899	4.7	2,088	2.8
1992	126	0.3	1,881	4.7	2,007	2.7
1993	189	0.5	1,287	3.2	1,476	1.9
1994	63	0.2	2,838	7.1	2,901	3.8
1995	3,339	9.2	1,395	3.5	4,734	6.3
1996	5,097	14.1	6,273	15.7	11,370	15.1
1997	1,020	2.8	549	1.4	1,569	2.1
1998	486	1.3	894	2.2	1,380	1.8
1999	3,135	8.7	1,740	4.3	4,875	6.4
2000	5,361	14.8	6,177	15.4	11,538	15.3
2001	1,113	3.1	1,035	2.6	2,148	2.8
2002	846	2.3	1,521	3.8	2,367	3.1
2003	63	0.2	0	0.00	63	0.1
2004	1,332	3.7	4,404	11.0	5,736	7.6
2005	486	1.3	879	2.2	1,365	1.8
2006	471	1.30	1,035	2.6	1,506	1.9
2007	204	0.6	0	0.0	204	0.3
2008	1,599	4.4	690	1.7	2,289	3.1
2009	345	0.9	0	0.0	345	0.5
2010	0	0.00	0	0.0	0	0.00
2011	0	0.00	0	0.0	0	0.00
2012	408	1.1	0	0.0	408	0.5
2013	0	0.00	0	0.0	0	0.00
2014	690	1.9	NA	NA	NA	NA
2015	5,139	14.2	564	1.4	5,703	7.5
2016	1,473	4.1	1,269	3.2	2,742	3.6
2017	63	0.2	1,332	3.3	1,395	1.8
2018	2,256	6.2	1,128	2.8	3,384	4.5
Total	36,216	≈100	39,999	≈100	75,525	≈100
Mean	1,249		1,429		2,697	

Table 6.11 Summary of Taiwan-related images appearing in *Time* and *Newsweek* between 1990 and 2018

Measure	Time	Newsweek	Total	Difference in Frequency between Time and Newsweek	Difference (%)
Taiwan-related image frequency	235	283	518	*Newsweek+48*	*Newsweek+9*

Measure	Time	Newsweek	Total	Difference in Frequency between Time and Newsweek	Difference (%)
Taiwan-focused image frequency	171	218	389	*Newsweek+47*	*Newsweek+12*
Taiwan as cover page focus	6	10	16	*Newsweek+4*	*Newsweek+25*
Page space	36216	39999	76215	*Newsweek+3783*	*Newsweek+5*
Average difference	NA	NA	NA	NA	*Newsweek+12.8*

Table 6.12 Summary of space given to Taiwan-related images for select years between 1990 and 2018

Year	Greater Frequency of Taiwan-Focused Images	Cover Pages	Page Space	Agreement (Equal Image Frequency, Covers, or Page Space)
1990	*Time* *Newsweek*	–	–	1
1991	*Newsweek*	*Newsweek*	*Newsweek*	0
1992	*Newsweek*	–	*Newsweek*	0
1993	*Newsweek*	–	–	0
1994	*Newsweek*	*Newsweek*	*Newsweek*	0
1995	*Time*	*Time*	*Time*	0
1996	*Time* *Newsweek*	*Time* *Newsweek*	*Time* *Newsweek*	3
1997	*Time*	–	–	0
1999	*Time*	–	–	0
2000	*Time* *Newsweek*	*Time* *Newsweek*	*Time* *Newsweek*	3
2001	–	*Newsweek*	–	0
2002	*Time*	*Newsweek*	–	0
2004	*Newsweek*	*Newsweek*	*Time* *Newsweek*	1
2008	–	–	*Time*	0
2015	*Time*	*Time*	*Time*	0
2018	–	–	*Time*	0

Framing Taiwan Images

To determine how the two publications presented American perspectives on Taiwan and cross-Strait relations in their Asian editions in the peak years of 1996 and 2000, I examined their editorial cartoons and in-text photos in detail and briefly read the accompanying news articles and analyses. In four editorial cartoons published in *Time* in 1996, Taiwan was always shown in contrast to China and mostly as a military target. Taiwan's name appears on a Chinese missile in the March 18 issue (p. 13), and in the March 25 issue (p. 9), a Mainland Chinese wearing a Mao-era suit is shown carrying a missile to be placed in a Taiwanese ballot box. Another drawing appearing in the March 25 issue (p. 7) shows Taiwan President Lee Teng-hui surrounded by missiles and a dark dragon representing China. In the only 1996 drawing not containing a missile, Taiwan is shown as a tiny fish about to be swallowed by a much larger fish labeled "China" (September 2, p. 11). The only *Time* cover image for that year appeared on March 18—instead of showing a single missile that might be interpreted as a warning shot, multiple Chinese missiles are pointed at Taiwan in what clearly depicts a massive attack.

Newsweek cartoonists also relied on dragon and missile themes for drawings published in 1996. Instead of a large fish eating a small fish, a February 19 drawing (p. 7) shows a large dragon getting ready to consume a much smaller dragon. In a March 4 cartoon (p. 7), a customer sitting at a table in a (presumably Chinese) restaurant is about to be waited on by a fire-breathing dragon. A March 25 drawing (p. 7) shows a Mainland Chinese, again wearing a Mao-era suit, preparing a missile to be shot toward Taiwan as a provocation; in the background, there is a restaurant advertising its take-out service, a somewhat racist trope that has long been used to represent China. In its April 1 issue (p. 9), *Newsweek* showed President Lee Teng-hui smiling in the knowledge that he has the world's most powerful nation to offer protection should China attack Taiwan. In a cartoon appearing four years later (April 3, 2000, p. 11), a Taiwan citizen is shown throwing a ballot box toward a dragon image representing China—a visual portrayal of the romantic ideal that democratic values will always prevail over oppressive regimes.

Briefly reviewing the eight photos published on the covers of the two magazines in 1996 and 2000, three showed a smiling President Lee Teng-hui with the headings "Taiwan's Choice: Now that the voters have spoken, what will Lee say to Beijing?" (from *Time*); "After the landslide: Democracy wins big in Taiwan—how will Beijing react?" (*Newsweek*); and "Mr. Democracy/Taiwan: The political odyssey of Lee Teng-hui" (Newsweek). The photos selected to accompany the text stories displayed images suggesting either an inevitable military conflict between China and Taiwan, Taiwan's democratic development, or Lee Teng-hui and other political leaders—images that belied the complexity of cross-Strait relations, with the US standing in the background.

Regarding text reports and analyses found in issues published during the same years, the emphases were on China as a strong regional bully and Taiwan as a weak but democratic Asian beacon with the world's most powerful country as its protector. When describing China's missile capabilities, *Newsweek* used a fireworks image to label it as a "noisy threat" (February 5, 1996, p. 10) similar to "a tire blowing out" (March 18, 1996, p. 10). *Time* argued "What is happening off Taiwan is pantomime rather than confrontation" (March 25, 1996). *Newsweek* described Taiwan as having "survive[d] and prospered despite nearly 50 years of such bullying from the mainland" (March 18, 1996, p. 10). *Time* claimed that to some Americans, "Taiwan is the last anticommunist country in the world" and that China's bullying behavior "needs to be disciplined, not indulged" (March 25, 1996). Should a cross-Taiwan Strait military confrontation occur, *Newsweek* predicted that Taipei would likely win diplomatic support from most the world and immense arms shipments, if not manpower, from the United States (February 5, 1996, p. 10). Two weeks later *Newsweek* described the American government as already feeling the threat to "stir nervousness along the Pacific Rim" (February 19, 1996, p. 8), while *Time* focused on Washington's feelings of "grave concern" over the missile crisis (February 12, 1996, p. 18). According to Andrew Nathan, a well-known China expert from Columbia University, the best China policy for the US government is "strategic ambiguity"—that is, the US government should not feel pressured to indicate a clear preferences for China or Taiwan. *Time* described the term "grave concern" as "a purposely ambiguous statement that not only angers America's containment advocates but also frustrate[s] Beijing" (March 25, 1996, p. 16). *Newsweek* argued that "the sense of mutual hostility continues to grow, aided, perhaps, by the American policy of 'creative ambiguity' (that's diplomatese for fudge) in the region" (March 18, 1996, p. 10). *Time* saw a potential for ambiguity to "lead to miscalculations" (February 12, 1996) and therefore called for greater clarity and precision in a cross-Strait policy backed by US power (*Newsweek*, March 18, 1996, p. 13; *Time*, March 25, 1996, p. 16). According to Andrew Nathan, the Clinton administration did attempt to reassure Beijing in the period immediately following the missile crisis.[5] First, it assured Beijing that it would deter Taiwan from seeking independence, and second, the US State Department asked Taiwan and China to engage in talks aimed at establishing "interim agreements." In 2000, *Newsweek* called for a revamping of America's one-China approach (May 22, 2000) and for greater effort by China and Taiwan to create a peacemaking formula (July 10, 2000).

The 1995 election of Lee Teng-hui as Taiwan's first democratically chosen leader was a strong focus in both magazines, as was the 2000 election of the Democratic Progressive Party candidate Chen Shui-bian, which ended a 50-year period of single-party control. Both publications used the open elections as evidence that Taiwan and China could never be considered alike (*Newsweek*, March 27, 2000; *Time*, March 27, 2000). According to *Newsweek*, Taiwan "deployed an even more formidable weapon [than missiles]: the spectacle of a free people casting votes" (April 1, 1996, p. 14), which "peacefully transformed a repressive dictatorship in less than a decade" (April 8, 1996, p. 13). In 2000, *Newsweek* described Taiwan as "feisty, wealthy and preparing to elect a new president" (March 6, 2000, p. 22). The cover of the May 22, 2000, issue proclaimed a "Brave New Taiwan: A New Society is Born"; the accompanying article stated that "The Taiwanese have built a vibrant democracy" (p. 12). *Time* described Taiwan as presenting a "good, beefy, democratic message" (March 18, 1996, p. 16) and Taiwanese voters as sending "a resounding answer to Beijing's rockets" (April 1, 1996). In the March 6, 2000, issue, *Time* tried to explain the situation on the island from a distance: "It is all colorful stuff, part of the messy learning curve of democracy with a free press and the beginnings of political transparency and accountability." *Newsweek* did the same, arguing that "A favorite Asian intellectual parlor game—whether democracy and human rights are universal human values or 'Western' impositions— had taken a profound turn toward universality" (April 1, 1999, p. 24). *Time* suggested that Lee Teng-hui's election was problematic "not just for communists, but also for advocates of authoritarian 'Asian values' and others who consider democracy an alien, Western-imposed concept that has no place in Asia and can even impede economic development" (April 1, 1996, p. 18). *Newsweek* quoted James Lilley (a former US ambassador to China) as arguing that "Democracy cannot be threatened by force, and free-market prosperity cannot be disrupted in Taiwan" (March 18, 1996).

Conclusion

This chapter examined how *Time* and *Newsweek*, two influential American news magazines with Asian editions, used photographs and editorial cartoons to construct favorable images of Taiwan and its political leaders between 1990 and 2018. Those images and their accompanying articles and editorials presented Taiwan as an independent country, despite the US government's spoken support for a one-China policy that claims there is only one China, that it is the People's Republic of China and that Taiwan is a Chinese province. But while the US government has acknowledged the one-China policy, it has increased its military arms sales and other forms of support to Taiwan's democratically elected government and encouraged Taiwan's participation in international forums and organizations, drawing strong protests from Beijing.

Time and *Newsweek*'s views on Taiwan are quite similar in terms of supporting a strong American military presence and a commitment to defending the island should China attack it. Both magazines view Taiwan's adherence to democratic values and practices as sufficient for earning American support and protections. This is a view shared by the American government, the country's intellectual community, and the public in general. In return for the support it has already received, Taiwan is responding to American expectations by practicing values that the United States and other Western countries consider "universal": democratic elections, liberal and open markets, and human rights protections—all considered fundamental to Western multilateral relationality. By following practices associated with American multilateral relationality, Taiwan can resist unilateral pressure from the Chinese government to engage in a bilateral relationality through which Beijing can exert greater pressure.

Notes

1 The 2018 end date was chosen due to the availability of circulation data online and in book form.
2 See David D. Perlmutter, *Visual Images and Foreign Policy: Picturing China in the American Press, 1949–1989*, Ph.D. dissertation (Minneapolis, MN: University of Minnesota, 1996).
3 *Baotu* is the Chinese translation of "thug."
4 See Perlmutter (1996), p. 260. The 20% standard and the method used in this chapter are both from Perlmutter's doctoral dissertation.
5 Andrew J. Nathan, "What's Wrong with American Taiwan Policy," *The Washington Quarterly*, 23(2) (Spring 2000), pp. 93–106.

7 In Lieu of a Conclusion
Five Implications

The goal for this book was to take a relational approach to understanding Taiwan's current status in the context of the changing dynamics of Sino–US relations—a purposeful attempt to step away from conventional and mainstream IR explanations that emphasize the factors of power or national interests, explanations that deny the ability of a small power like Taiwan to determine its future independent of the competition between China and the United States, currently the world's top two economic and military powers. According to the standard version of the power concept, it is normal to expect that nation-states will eventually engage in military conflict, since the pursuit of power, for whatever purpose, is a rational action based on perceived survival needs in an anarchical world—that is, in the absence of a centralized-power government. Alternately, the national interest concept teaches us that nation-states might not go to war if they see any possibility of working together, based on the belief that they are more likely to profit from collective action than from individual pursuits. This makes sense in an era of globalization, when economic achievements are more likely to attract the approval of domestic constituencies that vote for their political leaders—another instance of rationality, but based on economic interests. While these theoretical orientations view the nature of nation-states in different ways, they share a belief in an existing set of unwritten rules for state relations, with all states considered rational actors whose main (perhaps only) concerns are the pursuit of power and the protection of national interests.

This book offers an alternative view: a rising interest in the role of relationality rather than rationality, based on the perceived desire of all nation-states to pursue stable relations among themselves in the long run. This is especially true for states that rely on a different cultural or other habitus for relationship management. In these situations, it is also possible to use the constructivist IR concept to explain how actors in an emerging relationship must form a shared understanding or commonality in order for the relationship to continue, develop, or grow. A primary argument in this book is that

DOI: 10.4324/9780429486616-7

relationality involves identity building and that nation-states tend to move toward a consensus while creating imagined commonalties. Supporters of IR constructivism offer evidence in support of this assumption, arguing that nation-states participate in a continuous and intersubjective learning process. According to a relationality perspective, "relationship" is dialectical and therefore requires participating actors to manage their relationships rather than rely on a single actor. How such relationships will evolve is very difficult to predict—a starting point for this book's attempt to explain how China, the United States, and Taiwan can interact in a constituted way. Further, a relational approach helps us to understand how state relations are based on the identification and/or assignment of roles such as friend, enemy, competitor, rogue, great power, small power, beacon of democracy, dragon, and tiger. Each role contains social meanings that influence positive or negative feelings about others, as well as ways that states should interact with each other. In Chapter 6, I discussed how such a process of construction is possible for the United States and Taiwan—in fact, how it can serve as the foundation for current US–Taiwan relations.

In this book, I argued that if we want to understand Taiwan in the context of the changing dynamics of Sino–US relations, the relation concept deserves a position of centrality—the main motivating factor rather than power or self-interest for understanding state behaviors and interactions. This challenges the conventional view of states as units in an anarchic world rather than a social world in which states, like people, feel obligated in ways that contain or express social meaning.

Five implications can be drawn from the arguments presented in this book. First, Taiwan and the changing dynamics of Sino–US relations involve at least three types of relationality, one based on an ontological view, another on an epistemological view, and the third on an imitated view. The ontological view may be understood from a Chinese IR perspective that assumes that all states "under *tianxia*" ("under heaven") were born to be related, even though all states are not the same. According to this world view, China's relations with others should be considered bilateral relationships within a "greater-self," one based on certain obligations and commonalties that China might need to enforce unilaterally. In contrast, the epistemological perspective can be understood in terms of Western global governance practices in which all participating states are required to follow rules (sometimes stipulated, sometimes not) in order to be considered "related" to other states. This type of relationship-making is constructed on multilateral frameworks considered "universal"; therefore, exceptions are not to be considered or tolerated. The imitated view emerges from an analysis of Taiwan, a small power without the capability to determine the type of relationality it shares with China. However, by appropriating the most useful ideas from both Chinese and American culture, Taiwan can resist the imposition of a bilateral relationality even though it is not able to participate in the multilateral community dominated by the United States and other Western countries. When talking about Taiwan and the changing dynamics of Sino–US relations, we are actually talking about clashing visions of relationality. When China makes calculated decisions for its interactions with established international institutions, it knows that it will be the target of criticism and perhaps punishment from the established order. Currently, the United States is still the primary defender of the established system, which is why it is willing to support Taiwan's decades-long effort to become "the beacon of democracy in Asia." In return, Taiwan is receiving the rewards of close relationships with other members of established international society in addition to the United States.

Second, while Taiwan and the changing dynamics of Sino–US relations involve aspects of unilateral, bilateral, and multilateral relations, this book primarily focused on bilateral relations. At the unilateral level, actors can use whatever advantages they enjoy to execute actions in the interest of advancing their own security positions within established relational frameworks. In a unilateral context, a state can decide to take the first step toward making some kind of relational development possible. For example, a strong state like China or the United States might initiate an action or policy aimed at expressing good intentions in order to build or maintain a stable relationship, but it is also possible for one or the other to initiate a sanction to force the other side to make a relational adjustment. At the bilateral level, each relationship in the Sino–US–Taiwan triad is unlikely to resemble the other two (since each one is always involved in dialectic, processual, or continuous development), but any one of the bilateral relations will clearly be influenced by developments in the other two. Finally, according to a multilateral framework, individual actors are constrained or empowered by multilateral rules that determine positive and negative relations within a larger community.

Third, relations among Taiwan, China, and the United States involve a long-term need for relationship building and maintenance, and it is unlikely that any of the three are thinking in myopic terms of only caring about its own short-term benefits at all times. All states, even great powers, do care about their long-term relations, but relational stability receives little attention in the IR literature. The pursuit of long-term relations can take on different forms such as establishing economic partnerships or continuously creating imagined commonalties. However, in the triad that is the focus of this book, Beijing insists on fealty to the one-China principle to maintain stable relations with both the United States and Taiwan, both of whom are concerned about destroying or amending their current relations with China in order to establish new ones. In practical terms, the United States and Taiwan are refusing to get involved in the relationships that China is setting up, raising multiple questions concerning how to address and resolve different expectations.

Fourth, a relational approach may counteract the great power or asymmetrical power argument about the inevitability of conflict between a rising power and established superpower or about the hopelessness of a small power to have any leverage ("agency" in postcolonialist discourses) for influencing larger powers, whether those larger powers are viewed as threats or protectors. According to a relational framework, Taiwan can continue to reject pressure to repatriate, and China has other options besides military threats to encourage Taiwan to accept the one-China principle, or at least to discuss the issue at the negotiating table.

Finally, efforts to maintain relations do not guarantee a harmonious result. A relational approach to studying international politics and state behaviors does not entail a belief that when a state cares about maintaining long-term stability in its relations with others, that it will always take a harmonious approach rather than an antagonistic one. As discussed in Chapters 2 and 3, relationship building and maintenance requires trust and a shared consensus—both difficult to achieve. Relationships will continue to be aborted when one party tries to resist or punish another for purposes of achieving relationship expectations. In Chapter 4, I showed how China continues to resist what it views as acts of imperialism and hegemonism in the United Nations or from the United States—an example of negative relationship building. Another example is the Trump administration's attempt to decouple from China by pushing Beijing to reform its domestic market system in support of American corporations. A third example is Taiwan's attempt to decouple from Chinese culture when resisting Beijing's demands that it accept the one-China principle in order to gain greater independence. These negative and confrontational examples involve expectations for the emergence of new relations, perhaps of a different type. Power is an irrelevant factor in these situations—aborting relationships is not a practice limited to great or small powers.

Appendix
Individuals Interviewed for
This Book and Their Affiliations

Coen Blaauw, Executive Director, Formosan Association for Public Affairs. Interviewed on August 11, 2016, August 14, 2017, and July 15, 2019.

Dan Blumenthal, Senior Fellow and Director of Asian Studies, American Enterprise Institute. Interviewed on September 7, 2017.

Hal Brands, Distinguished Professor, School of Advanced International Studies, Johns Hopkins University. Interviewed on July 17, 2019.

David Brown, A China Studies Visiting Scholar at the School of Advanced International Studies, Johns Hopkins University. Interviewed on September 13, 2017.

Eric Brown, Senior Fellow, Hudson Institute. Interviewed on August 29, 2017.

Richard Bush, Nonresident Senior Fellow, Center for East Asia Policy Studies, the Brookings Institute. Interviewed on July 20, 2016, August 8, 2017, and July 22, 2019.

Ling Chen, Assistant Professor of Political Economy, School of Advanced International Studies, Johns Hopkins University. Interviewed on July 18, 2016.

Seth Cropsey, Senior Fellow & Director, Center for American Seapower, Hudson Institute. Interviewed on July 20, 2016, August 11, 2017, and July 9, 2019.

Robert Daly, Director, Kissinger Institute on China and the United States, Wilson Center. Interviewed on August 16, 2016.

Collin Davenport, Assistant to Republican Congressman Jerry Connolly. Interviewed on August 23, 2016.

Bruce Dickson, Professor of Political Science and International Affairs, The George Washington University. Interviewed on July 25, 2019.

Ian Easton, Senior Director, Project 2049 Institute. Interviewed on July 14, 2016, August 17, 2017, and August 1, 2019.

Michael Fonte, Director, Taiwan DPP Mission. Interviewed on August 15, 2016, and August 15, 2017.

Bonnie S. Glaser, Senior Adviser, Center for Strategic & International Studies (CSIS) [Mrs. Glaser now is the Director of Asia Program at the German Marshall Fund of the United States]. Interviewed on August 8, 2016, August 14, 2017, and August 8, 2019.

Charles Glaser, Professor of Political Science and International Affairs at the George Washington University. Interviewed on July 28, 2016.

Shihoko Goto, Deputy Director for Geoeconomics and Senior Associate for Northeast Asia, Asia Program, Wilson Center. Interviewed on July 14, 2016.

Michael J. Green, Senior Vice President for Asia and Japan Chair at the Center for Strategic and International Studies. Interviewed on August 31, 2016.

Rupert J. Hammond-Chambers, President, US Taiwan Business Council. Interviewed on August 7, 2019.

Harry Harding, Professor of Public Policy, University of Virginia. Interviewed on September 2, 2016.

Jim Heller, Director, Office of Japanese Affairs, US State Department. Interviewed on July 31, 2019.

Nong Hong, Executive Director and Senior Fellow, Institute for China-America Studies. Interviewed on September 13, 2017.

Russell Hsiao, the Executive Director of Global Taiwan Institute. Interviewed on July 27, 2016, and August 25, 2017.

Scott Kennedy, Senior Adviser and Trustee Chair in Chinese Business and Economics, Center for Strategic & International Studies (CSIS). Interviewed on August 16, 2017, and August 15, 2019.

David Lampton, Professor Emeritus of China Studies at the School of Advanced International Studies, Johns Hopkins University. Interviewed on August 8, 2016.

Susan Lawrence, Specialist in Asia affairs, Congress of Library. Interviewed on August 25, 2016.

Walter Lohman, Director of Asian Studies Center, Heritage Foundation. Interviewed on September 12, 2017, and July 18, 2019.

Tiffany Ma, Senior Director, National Bureau of Asian Research. Interviewed on August 18, 2016, and August 31, 2017.

Mark Manyin, Specialist in Asia affairs, Congress of Library. Interviewed on August 25, 2016.

Mike McDevitt, Senior Fellow, Center for Naval Analyses (CAN). Interviewed on August 5, 2016.

Liselotte Odgaard, Senior Fellow, Hudson Institute. Interviewed on August 5, 2019.

Douglas H. Paal, Nonresident Scholar, Asia Program, Carnegie Endowment for international Peace. Interviewed on July 25, 2016, August 15, 2017, and July 30, 2019.

Jonathan D. Pollack, Nonresident Senior Fellow, Center for East Asia Policy Studies, Brookings Institution. Interviewed on July 5, 2016.

Alan D. Romberg, Distinguished Fellow, Stimson Center. Interviewed on August 10, 2016, and September 7, 2017.

Stapleton Roy, Distinguished Fellow, Kissinger Institute on China and the United States, Wilson Center. Interviewed on July 21, 2016, August 10, 2017, and July 26, 2019.

Derek Scissors, Senior Fellow, American Enterprise Institute. Interviewed on July 25, 2019.

David Shambaugh, Gaston Sigur Professor of Asian Studies, Political Science & International Affairs and Director of the China Policy Program, The George Washington University. Interviewed on September 1, 2016.

Robert Spalding, Senior Fellow, Hudson Institute. Interviewed on July 15, 2019.

Mark Stokes, Executive Director, Project 2049 Institute. Interviewed on July 12, 2016, and July 11, 2019.

Yun Sun, Senior Fellow, the Stimson Center. Interviewed on September 6, 2017.

Robert Sutter, Professor of Practice of International Affairs, the George Washington University. Interviewed on July 26, 2016, August 28, 2017, and August 20, 2019.

Dennis Wilder, Managing Director and Senior Fellow, Initiative for US-China Dialogue on Global Issues at Georgetown University. Interviewed on August 3, 2016.

Joel Wuthnow, Research Fellow, Center for the Study of Chinese Military Affairs. Interviewed on July 16, 2019.

Guo-qing Zhen, Secretary at the Taipei Economic and Cultural Representative Office in the US. Interviewed on July 21, 2016.

Index

Note: Page numbers in *italics* indicate a figure and page numbers in **bold** indicate a table on the corresponding page. Page numbers followed by "n" indicate a note.

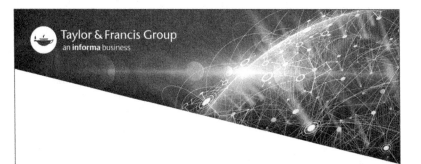

Printed in the United States
by Baker & Taylor Publisher Services